# Praise for *Google Analytics*™ *Integrations*

"Integrations are among the most important value-adds that Google Analytics provides, making it possible to combine both pre-visit and visit data to paint a complete end-to-end picture of a visitor's journey through a business. Integrations provide several kinds of important insights/analysis, ranging from deep insights into what ads lead to high quality traffic (e.g., AdWords integration) to how to better monetize your content (e.g., AdSense integration). Daniel is one of the best people to educate folks on the value and power of these integrations. I have known Daniel for several years, and he is easily among the most knowledgeable people I know when it comes to Analytics. He has worked closely with several businesses and publishers and helped them succeed, and it is great to get these deep insights directly from him."

—Sagnik Nandy, Distinguished Engineer, Google Analytics

"Daniel's insightful recommendations on how to make digital analytics more actionable via integration are well researched and tightly presented in this wonderful book. This is a must-read for analytics users and marketers!"

—Babak Pahlavan, Director of Product Management, Google Analytics

"A key benefit of Google Analytics is the deep integration with other Google products. Daniel does a great job of describing why the integrations are important, how to set them up, and how to actually use them."

—Justin Cutroni, Analytics Evangelist, Google Analytics

"Delivering on the promise of big data requires not just capturing massive amounts of data in individual silos, but also an incredible ability to integrate the aforementioned silos to let real insights transform businesses. Daniel's new book outlines specific strategies to accomplish this lofty goal for your digital data!"

—Avinash Kaushik, Author, *Web Analytics 2.0* and *Web Analytics: An Hour A Day*

# Google Analytics™
# Integrations

# Google Analytics™ Integrations

Daniel Waisberg

**Google Analytics™ Integrations**

Published by
John Wiley & Sons, Inc.
10475 Crosspoint Boulevard
Indianapolis, IN 46256
www.wiley.com

Copyright © 2015 by John Wiley & Sons, Inc., Indianapolis, Indiana

Published simultaneously in Canada

ISBN: 978-1-119-05306-4
ISBN: 978-1-119-05313-2 (ebk)
ISBN: 978-1-119-05325-5 (ebk)

Manufactured in the United States of America

10 9 8 7 6 5 4 3 2 1

For general information on our other products and services please contact our Customer Care Department within the United States at (877) 762-2974, outside the United States at (317) 572-3993 or fax (317) 572-4002.

Wiley publishes in a variety of print and electronic formats and by print-on-demand. Some material included with standard print versions of this book may not be included in e-books or in print-on-demand. If this book refers to media such as a CD or DVD that is not included in the version you purchased, you may download this material at http://booksupport.wiley.com. For more information about Wiley products, visit www.wiley.com.

**Library of Congress Control Number:** 2015936338

*To my parents, Sinai and Sonia,*
*who have always been a superb example to follow.*

# About the Author

**Daniel Waisberg** is an Analytics Advocate at Google, where he fosters Analytics by educating and inspiring professionals when it comes to data-driven decision making. He also spends a considerable amount of time analyzing and visualizing data to come up with interesting and actionable stories. Daniel is part of the Google Analytics Education team, and he also works closely with the Product and Marketing teams.

Daniel is the Founder & Editor of `http://online-behavior.com`, a respected Analytics and Optimization portal. Before joining Google he was a Google Analytics Certified Partner for more than 5 years, during which he had the opportunity to work with dozens of companies to help them measure, understand, and optimize their businesses in a more data-driven way.

Daniel holds a M.Sc. in Operations Research from Tel Aviv University, where he developed a statistical model to help optimize websites using Markov Chains. During those years he also developed a deep appreciation for people who understand statistics and use it to make better decisions.

You can read more about Daniel on his personal website, `http://danielwaisberg.com`.

# Credits

**Acquisitions Editor**
Mariann Barsolo

**Project Editor**
John Sleeva

**Technical Editor**
Deepak Aujla

**Production Manager**
Kathleen Wisor

**Copy Editor**
Kezia Endsley

**Manager of Content
Development & Assembly**
Mary Beth Wakefield

**Marketing Director**
David Mayhew

**Professional Technology & Strategy
Director**
Barry Pruett

**Business Manager**
Amy Knies

**Associate Publisher**
Jim Minatel

**Project Coordinator, Cover**
Brent Savage

**Cover Designer**
Michael E. Trent/Wiley

**Cover Image**
@iStock.com/Kenneth Drysdale

# Acknowledgments

First and foremost, I would like to thank four people who have been a source of inspiration and knowledge for many years: Justin Cutroni, Avinash Kaushik, Sagnik Nandy, and Paul Muret. I feel extremely honored and lucky to have the opportunity to work closely with these four gentlemen; in addition to contributing to my personal development, they have built much of the Web Analytics industry as we know it.

I would like to acknowledge the important help of Deepak Aujla, a Program Manager in the Google Analytics team and the Technical Editor of this book; he reviewed every chapter and provided insightful feedback on the content.

I would also like to thank a few Product Managers and Engineers at Google who reviewed the text for accuracy and completeness.

- Matt Matyas, Joan Arensman, and Dan Stone reviewed the "AdWords Integration" chapter.
- Kyle Harrison reviewed the "AdSense Integration" chapter.
- Fontaine Foxworth and Rahul Oak reviewed the "Mobile Apps Integrations" chapter.
- Erez Bixon and Michael Fink reviewed the "Webmaster Tools Integration" chapter.

My warm acknowledgements to the good people at Wiley, especially my editors, John Sleeva, Marian Barsolo, and Jim Minatel, who were always ready to accommodate all requests and did such a great job editing the book. And thanks to Knibbe Willem, who presented me to them.

This book was greatly enhanced by a few outstanding Analytics practitioners and thought leaders who contributed their knowledge and experience to several chapters. You will find their names close to their contributions throughout the book, but here is a list: Yehoshua Coren, Corey L. Koberg, Kristoffer Olofsson, Benjamin Mangold, Jim Gianoglio, Stéphane Hamel, and Peep Laja. Thank you very much. You guys rock!

# Contents at a Glance

# Contents

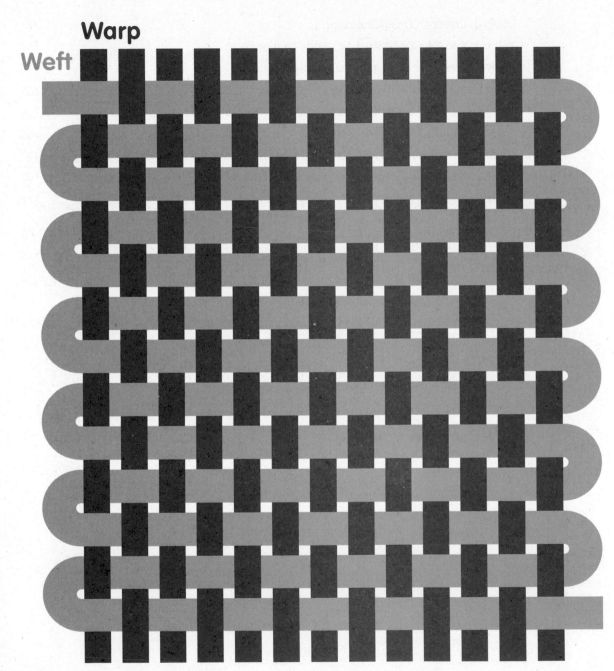

Warp

Weft

Illustration by Daniel Bronfen

# Introduction

Thousands of years ago, our ancestors understood the power of weaving flax fibers in a way that would turn long, disparate threads into cohesive pieces of cloth that could be used to warm and protect them. The process has changed along the years; we now have large and complex machines to do the work for us. The main principle is still very similar: A series of parallel threads (warps) is interwoven by another thread (weft) and pressed together.

This book similarly shows that Google Analytics can work very effectively as the weft that interweaves all your data sources, bringing them together as a whole in a cohesive data platform. Very often, you find data all over a company, but data sources run separate from one another, parallel as the warps in a loom, and integrating them may seem like an impossible endeavor. But it shouldn't be like that; all your data should be as tightly integrated as pieces of cloth.

The word *integration* comes from the Latin word *integratus*, past participle of *integrare*, which means to "make whole." In that sense, we can define *integration* as the process of bringing together parts or elements and combining them into a whole. When it comes to the world of data, integration means combining all the data you have about one entity (a user, a campaign, a product, and so on) in a single place.

Using Google Analytics, you can integrate data from other Google products to be viewed alongside its reports; you can also integrate other sources of data through custom integrations (provided that you have a *key* to join them together). This means that instead of having to analyze data using several different tools, you have the power to centralize all relevant information into Google Analytics to make data analysis easier and quicker. Analyzing data generated by different products in one central place will also result in more meaningful and actionable analyses.

Many professionals are still analyzing only a single part of their users' interactions with their digital properties. They can't see all the factors (and data) that affect their business, online and offline. This happens mainly because data is scattered over multiple tracking tools, making it hard for professionals to integrate all sources of information in one place. As you will learn in this book, Google Analytics is an extremely good candidate for creating an analytics platform that will centralize the most essential pieces of information for anyone working online.

In summary, this book is a hands-on guide focusing on one very important thing, which I personally believe to be critical for success: integrating all your data into Google Analytics so that you can have a full picture of your marketing efforts and your users' behavior. This quote from a research paper by Econsultancy is clear and to the point (see http://goo.gl/VFFHKD):

*"Integrating additional data into your web analytics provides a more complete vision of the entire marketing funnel. Your capability instantly expands from counting site traffic into a broader system that measures your effectiveness in advertising, sales online and offline, product usage, support, and retention."*

# Who Needs Google Analytics?

To put it simply: every business on the Web! While this might sound like an exaggeration, very few professionals would disagree with the claim that Web Analytics is essential to succeed in the digital world. Google Analytics is a robust and comprehensive solution, which can be implemented to answer the needs of small bloggers, larger-scale websites, and mobile apps.

While large enterprises typically employ analysts and experienced online marketers, small businesses usually have Google Analytics implemented by a Jack-of-all-trades. So even though this book includes technical terms, I have attempted to explain the subject in a clear and down-to-earth manner, with screenshots that support the written explanations. Hopefully, both experts and occasional Google Analytics users can learn from the tips and tricks presented here.

# Who Should Read This Book?

One of the important advantages of Google Analytics over other analytics solutions is the large and active user community on the Web, from forums to blogs to social networks. There is a vast amount of information on how to use and troubleshoot the tool. The aforementioned comes in addition to the official Google channels: Help Centers, Developer Documentation, Analytics Academy, and social channels. (See the links in the sidebar at the end of this section).

With that in mind, you might be asking yourself, "*Why do I need this book?*" That's a great question; thanks for asking!

Basically, this book centralizes everything you need to know about integrating data into Google Analytics, with detailed explanations and screenshots to guide you through this journey. In addition, the book is full of tips and tricks I've learned from many years of hands-on experience (I had a website running Google Analytics a month after it was launched in 2005!). So while some of the information will be available online, you will learn quite a few new tricks from this book!

Please note that while I provide links throughout this book to the Google Analytics Help Center and Developer Documentation, those links are largely here to help readers with specialized needs. Indeed, one of the advantages of using this book as a guide is that you don't have to go through all the details that aren't relevant to your particular situation. Instead, you'll be directed to the specific resources you need at the moment in the process you need them.

**CHECK OUT THESE RESOURCES TO GET THE MOST OUT OF THIS BOOK**

Google Analytics is a robust platform that can be used by people just starting their Analytics journey as well as by the most advanced Analytics geeks. But there are a few concepts and resources that are extremely important to understand before you start. Luckily, there is plenty of educational material to get you up and running. Here is a short list you might want to check before, after, or during the time you spend with this book.

- **Analytics Academy:** This is certainly the best resource to learn Google Analytics available in the Milky Way. (I haven't gone beyond that!) It contains many courses, from basic to advanced and from technical to business oriented. Check out `http://goo.gl/k9ejPt`.
- **Accounts, Users, Properties, and Views:** Every Google Analytics Account can be divided into *properties*, which can be divided into *views*. *Users* can have different access levels based on this hierarchy. It is important to understand how your account is structured; check out `http://goo.gl/A3lPhv`.
- **Universal Analytics:** Throughout the book you will encounter examples using the Universal Analytics code only (`analytics.js`). If you are not acquainted with this term or if you are still considering the upgrade, make sure to read `http://goo.gl/X9jJOA`.
- **Dimensions and Metrics:** In this book, you learn about dozens of metrics and dimensions, including how to organize them into reports and how to use them to analyze data. Make sure you understand their meaning; check out `http://goo.gl/1dEv74`.
- **The Interface Map:** This is a great visual summary of the Google Analytics interface. It will help you understand the names and locations of the capabilities offered by the tool; see `http://goo.gl/PXjFel`.

# How This Book Is Organized

During the writing process, this book's table of contents went through various iterations, mainly because there are many different ways to view the relationships between Google Analytics and other data sources. One hard decision I made was to include only the standard integrations that bring data *into* Google Analytics.

The reason behind this choice is that this book is intended to help any business use Google Analytics as a centralized data analysis platform. *But please don't get me wrong!* Integrations that are used to export data out of Google Analytics are also absolutely amazing, and they can be used to create powerful and customized solutions to businesses. They are just not in the scope of this book.

Since integrations are not that useful if the underlying data is inaccurate, I decided to start with an introductory chapter about implementation best practices. This chapter provides the most important information you need to know when implementing Google Analytics.

Following the chapter on implementation best practices, the book is structured in two main parts. Part I, "Official Integrations," discusses the Google Analytics official integrations—AdWords, AdSense, Google Play, iTunes, Webmaster Tools, and YouTube. Part II, "Custom Integrations," discusses ways to bring custom data into Google Analytics, mostly using the Data Import feature and the Measurement Protocol.

## How to Contact the Author

In this book, I provide practical advice on integrating Google products and external data into Google Analytics, with detailed information and screenshots. As you probably know very well if you are reading this, the Google Analytics team is constantly improving the tool and adding new functionality to it, which means you might not see exactly what I saw when writing the book. If that is the case, feel free to send me a note through the contact form at `http://danielwaisberg.com/connect`.

# 1 Implementation Best Practices

*On two occasions I have been asked, "Pray, Mr. Babbage, if you put into the machine wrong figures, will the right answers come out?" I am not able rightly to apprehend the kind of confusion of ideas that could provoke such a question.*

—Charles Babbage, Passages from the Life of a Philosopher

Charles Babbage's quote is a succinct explanation of the term GIGO (garbage in, garbage out), which, in decision sciences, is commonly used to describe situations where inaccurate data is fed into a model, resulting in the production of equally inaccurate results. The same is true in this book's context: You must make sure you are collecting accurate data before you start using it.

In order to use Google Analytics as a decision-making tool, companies cannot afford to rely on partial, inaccurate, or otherwise misaligned data. Google Analytics must be set up properly to meet the measurement needs and business objectives of companies.

In this chapter you will learn some of the most important steps in order to have clean, organized, and accurate data. The chapter is divided in five sections, each representing a step when it comes to implementing Google Analytics in a website or app successfully:

1. **Understanding the web analytics process:** Before you implement Google Analytics, it is important to understand how the data will be used and how the collection and analysis of data relate to other business areas. This will help you decide on the data needs of your company and which metrics will be used to measure success.
2. **Implementing and customizing codes:** Once your data needs and success metrics are defined, you should start looking for the necessary Google Analytics customizations to implement on your website or app.
3. **Setting up the Google Analytics interface:** Following the code implementation, you will need to set up the Google Analytics interface to make sure it processes your data in the way you want.

4. **Tagging inbound traffic:** In order to accurately measure all your website or app traffic, especially marketing campaigns, you will need to tag inbound links with custom URL parameters called UTMs.

5. **Managing the implementation:** To ensure that your implementation is always tidy, you should always keep track of changes on your Google Analytics account.

Please note that this chapter does not intend to provide a comprehensive description of Google Analytics implementation methods and capabilities; rather, it focuses on the most important aspects required to build an accurate and organized data collection.

# Planning Your Implementation

The objective of web analytics is to improve the experience of online customers while helping a company to achieve its results; it is not a technology to produce reports and spill data. Web analytics is a virtuous cycle that should never start with data collection; collecting data is a means to an end.

The diagram in Figure 1-1 shows a process you can use to implement web analytics in your company. It is not *the* process; it is *a* process. Each company should find the process that works best for it, but this is a simple process that might work for you.

1. Start with a clear definition of business goals.
2. Build a set of key performance indicators (KPIs) to track goal achievement.
3. Collect accurate and complete data.
4. Analyze data to extract insights.
5. Test alternatives based on assumptions learned from data analysis.
6. Implement insights based on either data analysis or website testing.

**WEB ANALYTICS PROCESS**

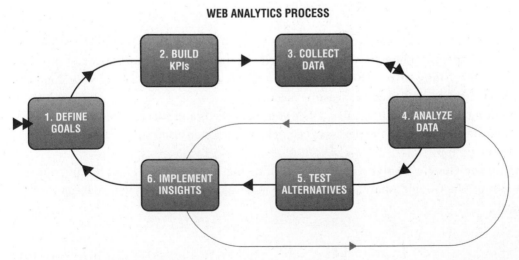

**Figure 1-1:** The web analytics process

This book focuses on steps three and four of the process in Figure 1-1: collecting and analyzing data. However, it is important to take a step back, before we dive into the bits and bytes of data, to remember that data should not live in a silo; it should be strongly linked to business and customer needs. Below you will learn a little about each of the steps shown in Figure 1-1. Following this section you will dive deeper into the technical aspects of Google Analytics implementation best practices.

## 1. Define Business Goals

This is the first step when it comes to understanding and optimizing a website or app: You must understand your business goals in order to improve it. The answer to the following question is critical in defining your goals: Why does your website or app exist?

Each website or app will have its own unique objectives. For some, the objective will be to increase pages viewed in order to sell more advertising (increase engagement); for others, the objective will be to decrease pages viewed because they want their visitors to find answers (increase satisfaction). For some, the objective will be to increase ecommerce transactions (increase revenue), and for others the objective will be to sell only if the product fits the needs of the customer (decrease products returns).

As you can see in the web analytics process proposed in Figure 1-1, the objectives are absolutely necessary in order to start the process. Only after they are defined can you proceed to build the KPIs. It is also very important to constantly revisit the goals in the light of website analyses and optimization to fine-tune them.

## 2. Build Key Performance Indicators

In order to measure goal achievement, you will need to create KPIs to understand whether the website results are going up or down. A KPI must be like a good work of art: It wakes you up. Sometimes it makes you happy and sometimes it makes you sad, but it should never leave you untouched, because if that is the case, you are not using the right KPIs.

And good works of art are rare. You have just a few truly touching works of art per museum, and not every work of art touches the same people. The same applies to KPIs. There are just a few truly good KPIs per company, and each person (or hierarchy level) will be interested in different KPIs—the ones that relate to their day-to-day activities. Upper-management will be touched by the overall achievement of the website's goals; mid-management will be touched by campaign and site optimization results; and analysts will be touched by every single metric in the world!

Good KPIs should contain three attributes:

- **Simple:** People in several departments with different backgrounds make decisions in companies. If KPIs are complex and hard to understand, it is unlikely that decision makers across the company will use them.
- **Relevant:** Each company has its unique objectives; therefore, it should also have its own set of KPIs to measure improvement.
- **Timely:** Even excellent KPIs are useless if it takes a month to get information when your industry changes every week.

By following the definition of the business objectives and the metrics that will be used to measure them, you will be in a much better condition to collect the data that will be needed.

## 3. Collect Data

When any company starts to collect website or app data, two questions should be asked:

- **Is my data accurate?** If your data is not accurate, it is like building an empire in the sand; your foundations can be shaken too easily.
- **Am I collecting all the data that I need?** If data is not collected, you will not be able to understand customer behavior properly.

You will learn more about Google Analytics data collection techniques in the following sections, so I will keep this step succinct.

## 4. Analyze Data

Data analysis is a rich field, which goes from simple filtering, sorting, and grouping to advanced statistical analysis. In this book you will learn about ways to analyze data using several Google Analytics reports and features, but the following are some general ideas that can help you go from data to insights:

- **Segment or die:** Segmentation is an essential technique when it comes to analyzing customer behavior. By segmenting your customers into meaningful segments, you will be able to optimize their experiences more easily and effectively.
- **Look at trends, not data points:** It is critical to look at your metrics over time to understand if the website results are improving or not.
- **Explore your data with visualization techniques:** You can chose from an endless pool of graphs and tools to visualize numbers. Exploring data with charts will uncover patterns and trends that are hard to find by crunching numbers.

It's important to note that data analysis can lead to three different outcomes (as shown in Figure 1-1):

- To discover an insight for implementation, such as a bug or a page that does not convert for an obvious reason.
- To develop a hypothesis regarding a low converting customer touch point that will lead to a split test.
- To come to an understanding of a data collection failure: Important data can be either missing or inaccurate.

# 5. Test Alternatives

There is an African proverb that says, "No one tests the depth of a river with both feet." In the same spirit, it is very unwise to change your website without first trying with the tip of your toes. When you test, you lower the risk of a loss in revenue due to a poor new design, and you bring science to the decision-making process in the organization.

But the most interesting outcome of experimenting is not the final result; it is the learning experience about your customers—a chance to understand what they like and dislike, which ultimately will lead to more or fewer conversions.

The web analyst must try endlessly and learn to be wrong quickly, learn to test everything and understand that the customer should choose, not the designer or the website manager. Experimenting and testing empowers an idea democracy, meaning that ideas can be created by anyone in the organization, and the customers (the market) will choose the best one; the winner is scientifically clear.

Following are a few tips when it comes to website testing:

- **Testing is not limited to landing pages:** It should be implemented across the website, wherever visitors are abandoning it and wherever the website is leaving money on the table.
- **Try your tools (and your skills) with a small experiment:** Sometimes it is wise to start small and then grow. Once you are familiar with your tools, try a test in an important page but for a small (or less profitable) segment. Then head for the jackpot!
- **Measure multiple goals:** While you improve macro conversions, you might be decreasing registrations or newsletter signups, which might have a negative impact in the long run.
- **Test for different segments:** Segments such as country and operating systems can have completely different behaviors, so the tests should also be segmented in order to understand those differences.

Google Analytics offers an A/B testing feature called Content Experiments; learn more about it at `http://goo.gl/HTGX2d`.

# 6. Implement Insights

No insight implementation is a synonym of no web analytics. If you go through all the preceding steps but cannot actually implement the results on your website, it is as if you did nothing. Following are some tips that can help you overcome implementation bottlenecks:

- **Get C-level support:** This will be essential if you come to a point where organizational priorities must be set and resources allocated.

- **Start small:** As mentioned previously, starting small helps to set expectations; people understand the tools and what is required from them.
- **Be friendly:** Being a nice person is always helpful; that's the way human nature works.

# Implementing and Customizing Your Code

If you are implementing Google Analytics for the first time, you will see a wizard that will guide you to retrieving the appropriate tracking code to use, right after creating an account. The first choice: what would you like to track, a website or a mobile app? If you choose a website, you will get a JavaScript code to implement on it; if you choose an app, you will get links to download either the Android or iOS SDKs.

If you miss the previous step or would like to find your tracking info at a later stage, you can find this page by logging into Google Analytics and clicking on Admin on the top of any page. This will lead you to the Administration panel where you can find an item named Tracking Info.

While implementing the default code on your website or app will provide you with important information about customer behavior, other code customizations might be required to accommodate your business needs. In the next section, I describe the customizations that I believe to be the most important; for a comprehensive and detailed description of all customizations available, visit `http://goo.gl/t1Td5T`.

---

**IMPLEMENTING GOOGLE ANALYTICS THROUGH GOOGLE TAG MANAGER**

If you are an experienced analyst/developer/marketer, you are probably asking yourself, "When is he going to start talking about Google Tag Manager?" A great question! In this chapter I focus my attention on the Google Analytics methods that should be used when enhancing your implementation, regardless of how you choose to actually implement them.

As you might already be aware, Google Tag Manager is a powerful and scalable way to organize your Google Analytics (and other tools) implementations. It will make updates easier and cleaner, and it will transform you into a hero. Here are a few resources you should consider when implementing Google Analytics through Google Tag Manager:

- The official Google Tag Manager Help Center: `http://goo.gl/1uXK90`
- The official Google Tag Manager Developer documents: `http://goo.gl/CPTYH6`
- Google Tag Manager Step-By-Step Guide (Web): `http://goo.gl/1BiX6t`
- Guide to Google Tag Manager for Mobile Apps: `http://goo.gl/ib3LL7`

# Cross Domain Tracking

If you would like to measure multiple websites that are linked together within a single Google Analytics property, it is important to adjust the code with Cross Domain Tracking (tracking behavior across subdomains does not require additional configuration). Failing to take into account multiple domains when implementing Google Analytics can significantly decrease data accuracy. Common cases are ecommerce carts, which are sometimes hosted on different domains; if the tracking code is not set up correctly in such instances, you might see a large number of direct or self-referral sessions ending on a transaction.

In order to understand Cross Domain Tracking thoroughly and grab the necessary codes for implementation, I recommend reading through both the Developer documentation at `http://goo.gl/5JvxJl` and the Help Center at `http://goo.gl/TJOWfp`.

# Enhanced Ecommerce

If your website or app offers merchandise or another type of ecommerce transaction, it is critical to implement the Google Analytics Enhanced Ecommerce functionality so that you can understand your customer journey better. This feature will enable you to have a deeper understanding of shopping behavior, campaign ROI, customer lifetime value, and other important information.

For a business and technical overview of the Enhanced Ecommerce feature, read `http://goo.gl/th9Roy`.

# Custom Dimensions

Creating audience segments is one of the most important techniques when trying to understand and optimize customer behavior; it allows you to make your website or app more relevant to different groups of users. Google Analytics provides a powerful segmentation capability by default, using a multitude of metric and dimension combinations.

In addition to the default segments, Custom Dimensions allow you to add attributes of a user, session, or action when collecting data. For example, a business that sells different types of memberships should be able to understand how each member type behaves; a large publisher should be able to understand how each of their authors is performing; and a travel website should be able to know which kind of hotel their returning customers like the most.

You will learn more about Google Analytics Segments and Custom Reports throughout the book. However, the subject is especially important when it comes to Custom Dimensions, as those dimensions do not appear in any of the standard reports. Therefore, the best ways to analyze behavior based on Custom Dimensions are as follows:

1. **Create a segment:** The Segment builder enables you to create a segment that includes or excludes the behavior of specific users. For example, you might want to exclude from your

reports all your existing clients (defined through a Custom Dimension) using a segment. This would be wise when analyzing customer acquisition efforts. You might also want to include in your reports only users who are part of your loyalty program (defined through a Custom Dimension) to analyze what type of content they are most interested in. Those are only two examples; to learn more about creating segments, visit `http://goo.gl/6gbC2k`.

2. **Build a Custom Report:** Google Analytics allows its users to create Custom Reports using the metrics and dimensions available in the tool to tailor their reports to their business needs. This functionality can be used to build reports including Custom Dimensions and acquisition behavior, or conversion metrics that can help you understand your users' behavior. To learn more about Custom Reports, visit `http://goo.gl/eOADkr`.

For a detailed explanation on why and how to use Custom Dimensions, read `http://goo.gl/fvhL8L`.

## Download Clicks

Different websites have different goals. You learned previously about a way to measure ecommerce transactions, and you will learn shortly about a way to measure advertising revenue through the AdSense integration, but some websites will have downloads as their main goal. Google Analytics will not measure clicks on download links by default, so it is critical to add a customized code to your website if you are encouraging people to download any type of file. Here is a guide explaining how to do it: `http://goo.gl/uUm4rq`.

## Advanced Content Tracking

Every website owner should be able to understand how its users consume content. However, sometimes users behave in ways that cannot be measured by a default implementation. For example, when someone lands on a long article, reads through the whole piece, and then leaves the website, from a Google Analytics perspective, this person viewed just one page and didn't interact with the content. This is a problem when it comes to content publishers.

With that in mind, Justin Cutroni, Analytics Evangelist at Google, developed a script that sends events to Google Analytics whenever a user scrolls down a page. In addition, the script uses Custom Dimensions to categorize users into "scanners," users who scroll to the bottom of the content in less than 60 seconds, and "readers," users who take more than 60 seconds to reach the bottom of the content. This solution is excellent for measuring users' content consumption patterns. Read more at `http://goo.gl/21eIi0`.

## Troubleshooting Code Implementation

If you manage a website, it is critical to keep an eye open at all times to make sure your implementation is okay, especially when you update the website code. The following list of tools created by the Google Analytics team will help you with this task:

- **Diagnostics** (in-product feature): When you log in to your Google Analytics account and select a view, you will notice a bell icon in the upper-right corner of your page. You will also notice that sometimes there will be a notification number there. If you click on the bell, you will find a list of customized notifications for your code implementation and set up. Make sure you read through them and fix the issues. Learn more at `http://goo.gl/8NC2Y4`.
- **Real Time** (in-product feature): Google Analytics provides Real Time data for website behavior, where you can see what is happening right now on your website or app. This is very useful for website debugging, since you can make changes in the code and find out how they are affecting the data in real time.
- **Tag Assistant** (Chrome extension): This extension allows you to check your Google Analytics tag (and other Google tags) while browsing the website. It is a handy tool to check and troubleshoot implementations quickly. Download it from the Chrome Store at `http://goo.gl/P1LstJ`.
- **Google Analytics Debugger** (Chrome Extension): This extension provides more detailed and technical data (as compared to the extension) about what is being sent from a page to Google Analytics. Download it from the Chrome Store at `http://goo.gl/yn9dHj`.

## Setting Up the Google Analytics Interface

In this section you will learn some of the most important settings to help you create a clean Google Analytics account with a good level of data accuracy. For a comprehensive and detailed explanation of all possible tool settings, visit `http://goo.gl/2aWv9b`.

### Setting Up Goals

Goals are the soul of a Google Analytics account; no analysis will provide valuable insights if you do not measure your goals. Goals can be measured in multiple ways: an ecommerce transaction (see previous section), a thank-you page for a newsletter subscription, a session that lasted a certain time, a visit with a certain number of pages viewed, and others. In order to help website owners set up goals, Google Analytics provides a series of templates, as shown in Figure 1-2.

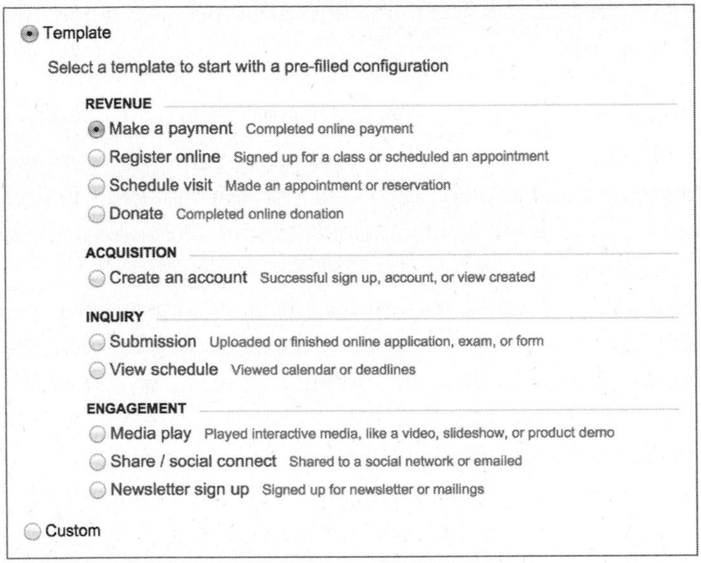

**Figure 1-2:**   Google Analytics goals templates

However, if you decide to create a custom goal based on your own needs, you can choose among four goal types:

- **Destination:** Triggered when a web page or app screen loads (e.g., reaching a "thank you" page).
- **Duration:** Triggered when a user stays on a website or app longer than a pre-defined amount of time in a single session.
- **Pages/Screens per session:** Triggered when a user views more than a pre-defined amount of pages or screens in a single session.
- **Event:** Triggered when an event is triggered by the user (e.g., clicking on a button or playing a video).

Use the following guide to learn more about why and how to set up goals: `http://goo.gl/YbDVqi`.

## Focusing on Potential Customers

Wide ranges of people may visit your website; unfortunately, that number includes employees of your own organization and service providers, neither of whom are the visitors you want to understand and optimize for. Therefore, it is important to create filters that exclude the IP range used by your organization and its service providers, such as web development and marketing agencies.

Google Analytics offers a series of predefined filters, where you will find an option to "exclude traffic from the IP addresses" (see Figure 1-3). This option is perfect if you want to exclude a simple range of addresses by using the "that begin with" or "that end with" options. If you want to filter a more complex range of IP addresses, check out `http://goo.gl/PSaL15`.

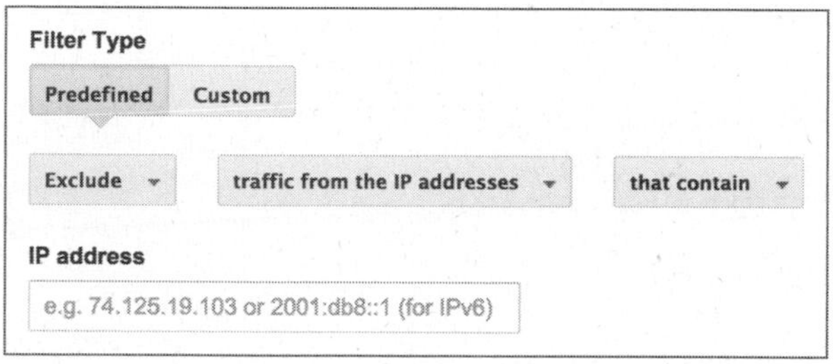

**Figure 1-3:** Predefined filter to exclude IP addresses

In addition, Google Analytics also offers the option to filter bot traffic. This filter will exclude all hits coming from the IAB known bots and spiders, allowing you to identify the real number of users who are coming to your site. To include the filter, visit your Administration panel and select a checkbox option available in the View Settings menu in the view you would like to filter; the option is labeled "Exclude all hits from known bots and spiders."

## Removing Parameters That Do Not Point to Unique Content

One of the interesting insights we can learn from Google Analytics is the navigation patterns between website pages; you can find this information in the Behavior section of Google Analytics standard reports. However, websites can use multiple URL parameters to refer to the same page and, by default, Google Analytics considers one page with multiple parameter values as multiple distinct pages. Therefore, if your content is not unique for these parameters, you should remove the duplicate pages from your reports.

Google Analytics provides a simple interface to exclude URL parameters from reports; under View Settings in the Administration Panel you will find a field called "Exclude URL Query Parameters." When you add a parameter to this field, GA will ignore the parameter, joining pages that might be considered separate.

## Eliminating Duplicate Pages

Google Analytics is case sensitive. This means that `example.com/HELLO` and `example.com/hello` would be recognized as two different pages, generating duplicate entries in your content reports. However, from a customer's perspective, those pages are usually the same. (Check if this is the case with your website before you create the following filter.) Therefore, it is important to lowercase all

URLs. Figure 1-4 shows an example of what this filter would look like. You can learn more about creating view filters at `http://goo.gl/VzefpJ`.

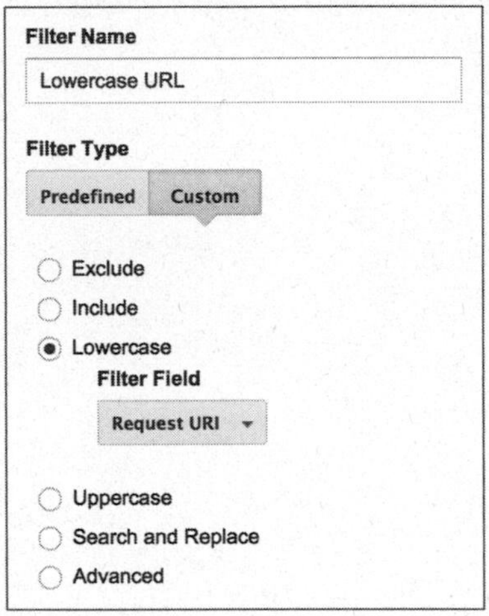

**Filter Name**

Lowercase URL

**Filter Type**

Predefined | Custom

○ Exclude
○ Include
◉ Lowercase
   **Filter Field**
   Request URI ▾

○ Uppercase
○ Search and Replace
○ Advanced

**Figure 1-4:** Filter to lowercase URLs

Because the same issue can affect other fields, especially campaign data, I also recommend creating lowercase filters for the following fields:

- Campaign name
- Campaign term
- Campaign medium
- Campaign source

## Setting Up Site Search

An excellent way to understand visitor intent is to study search terms used on the internal site search (search boxes located on the website that allow visitors to search the website content); they show what your visitors are looking for on the website.

A proper setup of the Google Analytics Site Search feature will help website owners understand which content is being searched for, which searches are yielding irrelevant results, and which ones are driving sales (or another goal) on the website. As shown in Figure 1-5, you will have the option to add up to five parameters to define a search and up to five parameters as a category. You will also be able to strip the parameters from this view (check the box below the text field), which works like removing the parameter, as explained above. Here is a guide on how to do it: `http://goo.gl/jvm8wu`.

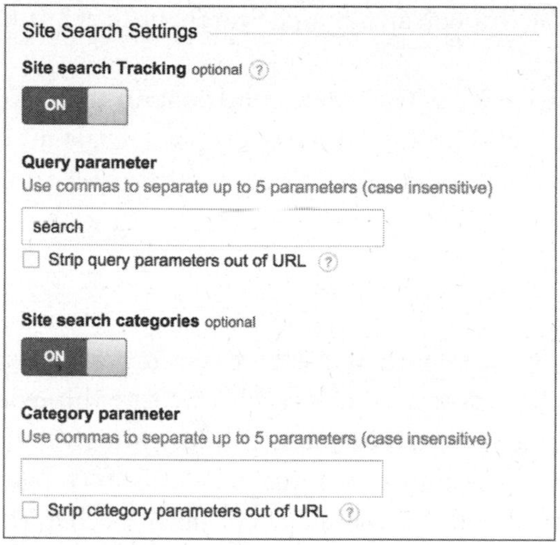

**Figure 1-5:** Setting up site search

## Enabling Display Advertising and Demographics Reports

Enabling both Display Advertising and Demographics and Interest Reports will bring a vast amount of insightful and actionable data into your reports. Once you enable them you will see behavior information relating to user age, gender, and interests. But even more importantly, this data can also be used to segment standard reports and create remarketing lists. (See Chapter 2, "AdWords Integration," for more on remarketing.)

The first step to enabling these reports is to update Google Analytics to support Display Advertising, which enhances data with the DoubleClick cookie information whenever it is present (for websites), or with the Advertiser ID when they are collected (for apps). To enable this setting, log in to Google Analytics and click on Admin at the top of your screen, choose the property you would like to enable, and click on "Property Settings." You will find an item named "Enable Advertiser Features." Please note that once you enable the advertiser features, you might be required to update your privacy policy. You can read more about this setting and its requirements at `http://goo.gl/ycVvpM`.

The second step, which can also be performed in the Property Settings, is to enable the Demographics and Interest Reports. Read more about why and how to enable this set of reports at `http://goo.gl/OwZpr4`.

## Excluding Referrals

This setting allows you to add domains to be ignored by Google Analytics as referrals. This means that a user who lands on your website from an excluded domain will be handled similar to

Direct traffic. If the user has previously visited the website through an Organic Search, he or she will still be attributed to Organic.

Google Analytics will add your own domain to this list by default (the same domain that you added to the Property settings). Another common use would be a third-party cart where the user is redirected to your website after a purchase or a sister website that should not count as a Referral.

# Tagging Your Inbound Traffic

Properly implemented, Google Analytics can help you with the important task of measuring customer acquisition campaigns. Google Analytics automatically detects when users reach a website through an Organic Search or Referral, but it won't know a user came from a newsletter unless you give it a way to detect that. The same happens to AdWords campaigns: unless you link AdWords to Google Analytics, you won't see accurate numbers on your reports; but this is the subject of an entire chapter. For now I will focus on other marketing platforms.

If you are sending newsletters, purchasing banner placements, or even advertising offline, it is important to use campaign tags properly. Google Analytics will show users coming from a billboard or a TV ad as Direct traffic; it can show visitors from newsletters as Direct, `mail.google.com`, or other email provider traffic; it can show visitors from banner campaigns as Direct, `ad.doubleclick.net`, or the website itself. These behaviors are clearly suboptimal when it comes to measuring campaign effectiveness.

For such cases, Google Analytics has developed a system for you to "tell" it if users came from a campaign: UTM parameters. (UTM stands for Urchin Traffic Monitor, a remnant of Urchin, the tool Google acquired in order to build Google Analytics.) Basically, the system allows you to construct links that convey specific information about how the visitor arrived at the website.

## Tagging Custom Campaigns

Using UTM parameters, you can create links that include five variables that, taken together, help Google Analytics "see" how users got to the website:

- `utm_source` describes the origin of the visitor. Since every visitor must come from some place, this is a required parameter. It is usually the URL of the website where the campaign is running, such as `theguardian.com`, `online-behavior.com`, `newsletter`, or others.
- `utm_medium` describes the channel used by the visitor; it is also a required parameter. It could be `cpc`, `display`, `social`, `email`, or others.

- `utm_name` describes the name of the campaign. It could be a special campaign such as "Launch," an ongoing campaign such as "Product X," or a newsletter edition such as "newsletter-jan-2015."
- `utm_term` describes the term clicked on in a campaign. It could be a search term or a term used in a newsletter. For example, if you are advertising on a search platform for the search terms "analytics" and "measurement," you would have the source `example.com`, the medium `cpc`, the name "Analytics Campaign," and the terms "analytics" and "measurement" for each ad.
- `utm_content` describes the version of an advertisement on which a visitor clicked. It is often used to analyze the effectiveness of banner design or copy in a campaign. For example, if you advertise on `cnn.com` and use two different banners, you would use the same parameters for source, medium, and name, but would add a unique value for each banner on the content UTM; this would enable you to learn which banner is better.

**NOTE**    Google has developed a tool in order to build links using these campaign variables called URL Builder. It can be accessed at `http://goo.gl/yQycsq`. In order to tag multiple URLs once, use the following template, created by Cardinal Path, a Google Analytics Certified Partner and Google Analytics Premium reseller: `http://c05tdu`.

If you have existing campaigns tagged with custom link parameters (different from the UTM), there is a way to translate them into UTMs without physically changing the campaign links, but this would require an addition to the GA tracking code. For technical implementation details, check the following plugin: `http://goo.gl/GytPhO`.

## Tagging FeedBurner Traffic

For content publishers, from individual bloggers to large content portals, Really Simple Syndication (or RSS) is a common way to inform readers of new posts/articles. RSS is a family of web feed formats used to publish frequently updated works, and FeedBurner is a tool provided by Google to create (or burn) website feeds.

To help publishers better understand traffic acquired through RSS, the FeedBurner team created a way to make sure that feed links are tagged properly with UTM parameters. This is important to have a better understanding of how and where readers consume your content.

In order to tag FeedBurner traffic, log in to your feed at `http://goo.gl/SuI6rx`. On the Analyze tab (the default), you will find a link on the left sidebar under Services named Configure Stats. Click on it and you will reach the screen shown in Figure 1-6.

As indicated by number 3, you will be given the option to Track Clicks as a Traffic Source in Google Analytics. Once you check the box to enable the tracking, click on Customize. You will see the screen shown in Figure 1-7.

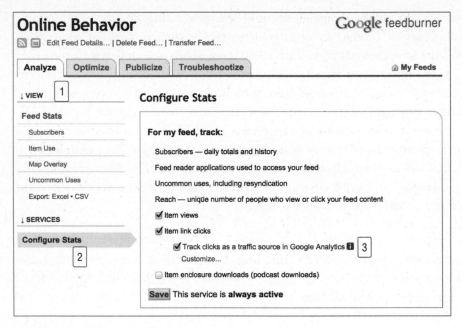

**Figure 1-6** Configuring FeedBurner links

**Customize Google Analytics Tracking**

Clicks on items in your FeedBurner feed will show up in Google Analytics under the "Traffic Sources" section. Customize how these clicks are displayed by editing the source, medium, campaign, content, and terms.

**Variables you can use**
(click to insert into the textbox with focus)

| | |
|---|---|
| Source | feedburner |
| Medium | ${distributionChannel} |
| Campaign | ${feedName} Feed |
| Content | ${distributionEndpoint} |
| Term | |

**${feedUri}**
Your feed's URI, e.g. Online-Behavior

**${feedName}**
Your feed's name, e.g. Online Behavior

**${distributionChannel}**
The channel in which your feed is distributed, e.g. feed, email

**${distributionEndpoint}**
The application where a click request originates, e.g. Google Reader, Gmail

Close

**Figure 1-7** Customizing FeedBurner links

FeedBurner allows you to use the following dynamic variables to populate the UTM parameters:

1. ${feedUri}: The feed URI
2. ${feedName}: The feed name

3. `${distributionChannel}`: The channel in which the feed is distributed, usually either feed or email
4. `${distributionEndpoint}`: The application where a click request originates, such as Gmail

Here is a suggestion of how you can set up the parameters in order to understand FeedBurner traffic in an effective way:

1. **Source**: `feedburner`
2. **Medium**: `${distributionChannel}`
3. **Campaign**: `${feedName} Feed`
4. **Content**: `${distributionEndpoint}`

Both Custom Campaigns and FeedBurner traffic discussed in this section can be found under the Acquisition tab on Google Analytics; to analyze a campaign search for it on the All Traffic report.

# Managing Your Implementations Effectively

Google Analytics implementations are a continuous process; there are always new features that require changes to the tracking code or to the account settings. In order not to lose control over what is and is not implemented, or when it was configured, you must be extremely organized. In this chapter, you will learn a method to avoid losing data and context on Google Analytics reports.

**NOTE** If you are not acquainted with the definitions of accounts, properties, and views, read `http://goo.gl/TAv93N` before proceeding. In addition, please note that when you create new views, they will start being populated from their creation date, even if another view in the property has been collecting data for longer than that.

## Creating Raw Data and Staging Views

The best way to check configuration errors is to have a view that does not use any filters. By comparing it to your main view, you will be able to quickly learn if you have a misplaced or problematic filter. Once you create this view, you should also set up the same goals you have in your main view. This will make the data more relevant in case you need to use it. For example, if you find out that your main view has a filter that affected your past data, you might want to use the Raw Data view for a while.

Suppose that you decide to create a filter to lowercase URLs (as proposed earlier), but you are uncertain about how it can affect your data. The best way to proceed is to have an additional view with the exact same settings as your main view and apply the new filter to the test view only.

Once the filter is applied, you can check the data and compare the numbers to learn if anything went wrong. (Tip: Wait for at least one full day of data, as filters might take 24 hours to start filtering data.) The following article shows how to add a new view: `http://goo.gl/wHHEuj`.

## Creating an Analytics Staging Property

If you have worked in the web analytics industry long enough, you have probably seen data corrupted as a consequence of bad implementations. Code changes should be undertaken with care. However, since code changes affect all views in a property, it is not effective to create a new view in this case.

Since most websites have a staging site where changes are tested before going live, I suggest having a different tracking code (that is, a new Google Analytics property) used for those environments to test code changes on the Google Analytics tracking code. Also make sure to have the same configurations on both properties. Learn how to set up a property at `http://goo.gl/VBkTkd`.

## Keeping Track of Implementation and Configuration Changes

Changes are constantly made to Google Analytics views by users as they refine their website goals, improve filters, take advantage of new features, and so forth. Every change may impact data, sometimes in unexpected ways. For this reason, it is essential to have a system in place to keep track of code and view changes, especially in large organizations where more than one person is involved with Google Analytics. But even when only one person is involved, this is important, as employees may go on leave, get promoted, or leave the company.

Google Analytics offers an out-of-the-box feature called Change History that includes changes made to your account settings, such as changes in goals, filters, and user permissions. As shown in Figure 1-8, apart from the change itself, you will see who did it and when. To find this report, log in to Google Analytics and click on Admin at the top of your screen; this setting will be available under your account settings.

| Date | ↑ | Changed By | Change |
|---|---|---|---|
| Jan 20, 2015, 11:09:44 PM | | | Filter "Amazing filter!" created |
| Jan 20, 2015, 11:09:44 PM | | | View "Testing profile" linked to filter "Amazing filter!" |
| Jan 9, 2015, 2:05:14 PM | | | AdWords link group "Online Behavior" created |

**Figure 1-8:** Change History table sample

In order to centralize the collection and sharing of the changes made to a Google Analytics account, including code changes, I propose using a Google Docs form. The form should be created so that all interested parties can be aware of all changes. These will then be saved for historical knowledge to be used by the whole team (and future team members). Figure 1-9 shows an example of such a form with fields that you might want to create.

**NOTE** You can learn how to build a Google Docs form at `http://goo.gl/1XKAkI`.

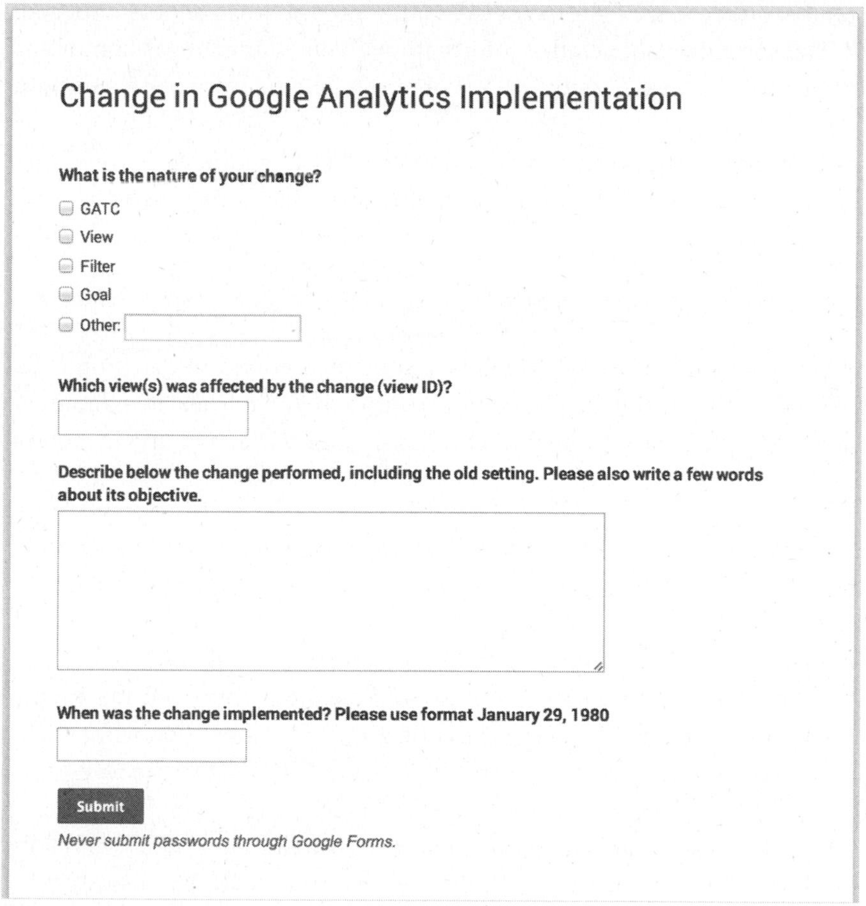

## Change in Google Analytics Implementation

**What is the nature of your change?**

☐ GATC
☐ View
☐ Filter
☐ Goal
☐ Other: [                    ]

**Which view(s) was affected by the change (view ID)?**

[                    ]

**Describe below the change performed, including the old setting. Please also write a few words about its objective.**

[                                        ]

**When was the change implemented? Please use format January 29, 1980**

[                    ]

[ Submit ]

*Never submit passwords through Google Forms.*

**Figure 1-9:** Tracking Google Analytics implementations using Google Docs

# Keeping Track of External and Overall Changes with Annotations

Google Analytics Annotations is a feature that allows you to annotate data points on the Google Analytics user interface, providing context when analyzing data, which allows for richer analyses. Here are some important occasions when you should use this feature:

- Offline marketing campaigns (radio, TV, and billboards)
- Major changes to the website (design, structure, and content)
- Changes to tracking (changing the tracking code and adding events)
- Changes to goals or filters

While annotations can (and should) be used for technical changes to the website, it is important to keep them at a high level. You shouldn't add detailed information about your changes or annotate relatively minor tweaks; otherwise the annotations will become too dense to convey meaningful information to readers.

The use of both methods described here (form and annotations) should create an optimal mix. Watch the following video to learn how to use the Annotations feature: `http://goo.gl/MiHVuH`.

## Summary

In this chapter you learned best practices for Google Analytics implementations and recommendations on how to best set the tool so that it collects clean and accurate data. You learned about the five major steps when it comes to implementing Google Analytics in your website or app in a clean, organized, and accurate way.

1. **Understand the web analytics process:** Before implementing Google Analytics, it is important to understand how the data will be used and how the collection and analysis of data relate to other business areas.
2. **Implement and customize codes:** Once your data needs are defined, you should start looking for the necessary Google Analytics customizations to implement on your website or app.
3. **Set up the Google Analytics interface:** Following the code implementation, you will need to set up the Google Analytics interface to make sure it processes your data in the way you want.
4. **Tag inbound traffic:** In order to accurately measure all your website or app traffic, especially marketing campaigns, you will need to tag inbound links with custom URL parameters called UTMs.
5. **Manage the implementation:** To make sure your implementation is always tidy, you should always keep track of changes on your Google Analytics account.

In the next chapters you will learn how to integrate Google tools into Google Analytics in order to enhance your data and create a powerful, data-driven decision-making tool. For each of the integrations you will learn how to integrate it into Google Analytics and how to use the resulting reports to analyze and optimize online behavior.

# Official Integrations

# 2

# AdWords Integration

*This chapter was co-written with Yehoshua Coren, Founder & Principal at Analytics Ninja LLC, a web analytics consultancy that provides advanced Google Analytics implementations and analysis for businesses large and small.*

Linking Google Analytics to AdWords is essential to professionals using both tools. It allows marketers and website owners to go beyond success and failure, to understand not only which campaigns are succeeding or failing, but also what happens to users who do not purchase anything (or complete any other goal) during their sessions. This information is critical to optimizing campaign performance by shedding light on which campaigns are failing as a result of suboptimal targeting, poorly designed landing pages, or poor ads. In addition, by importing AdWords data into Google Analytics, marketers can compare campaign traffic to other sources of traffic, understanding how each can be optimized for its strength.

In this chapter, you learn how to link AdWords to Google Analytics, which reports you get access to, and advanced analysis techniques to make the most of your AdWords campaigns.

## Integrating AdWords and Google Analytics

In this section, you learn about the process of linking and unlinking Analytics and AdWords accounts and how to configure your settings for better integration. Following that, you learn about some of the most common issues when comparing AdWords and Google Analytics data, including what can go wrong and how to fix it.

### Linking AdWords and Analytics

The following steps enable you to link accounts and configure reports in an organized and easy-to-understand way.

#### Step 1: Make Sure You Have the Necessary Access Levels

The first step to linking an AdWords account to Google Analytics is having the right access levels. The integration can be accomplished only if you have Edit access to a Google Analytics property and

Administrative access to an AdWords account. These links point to the relevant Help Center articles explaining how to grant the right access levels:

- Google Analytics: http://goo.gl/YD4WfS
- AdWords: http://goo.gl/SWmy6g

### Step 2: Find the Product-Linking Section and Choose the AdWords Account to Link

In order to link your Google Analytics and AdWords, log in to Google Analytics and click on Admin at the top of your screen. Then, choose the property you want to link to your AdWords account and look for a menu item named AdWords Linking or All Products.

**NOTE** The linking happens at the property level, but as you will learn, you can still make the data available at a view level.

If you have no AdWords accounts linked you will see a screen similar to Figure 2-1, where you will see the AdWords account(s) you have available for linking (those where you have Administrative access). If you have access to multiple AdWords accounts through a My Client Center (MCC), you will be able to link multiple accounts by checking them.

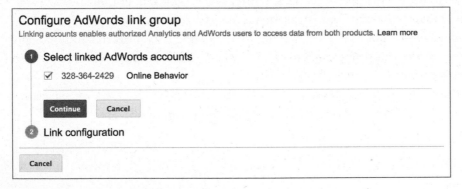

**Figure 2-1:** First step to linking AdWords

### Step 3: Choose Google Analytics Views to Link

After you click on Continue (the button that appears under your account number in Figure 2-1), you will be given the opportunity to choose which views in your property will show AdWords data in it. Figure 2-2 shows the Link Configuration step, where you can name your link group, which is a group of linked AdWords accounts, and choose the views that will receive data.

It is important to carefully choose which views will have access to AdWords data, as some of the Google Analytics users in your company might not be supposed to have access to AdWords data. When you choose a view, cost data will automatically be applied to it; that is, you will be able to see the actual cost of clicks and campaigns in those views.

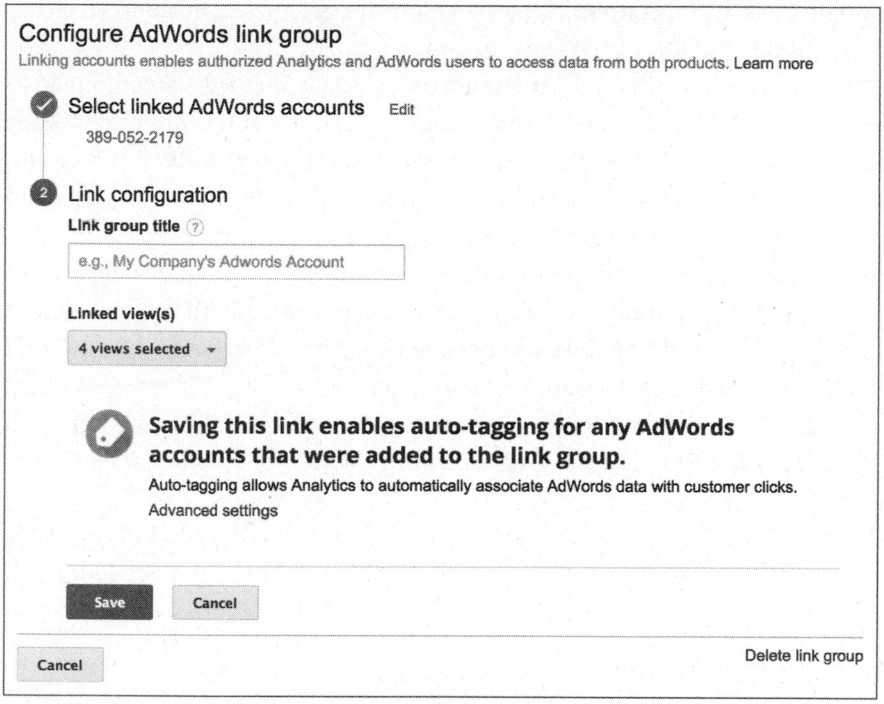

Configure AdWords link group

Linking accounts enables authorized Analytics and AdWords users to access data from both products. **Learn more**

✓ Select linked AdWords accounts    Edit
   389-052-2179

② Link configuration
   **Link group title** ⑦

   | e.g., My Company's Adwords Account |

   **Linked view(s)**

   | 4 views selected ▾ |

   ◔ **Saving this link enables auto-tagging for any AdWords accounts that were added to the link group.**
   Auto-tagging allows Analytics to automatically associate AdWords data with customer clicks.
   Advanced settings

   | Save |    | Cancel |

   | Cancel |                                    Delete link group

**Figure 2-2:** Choosing Google Analytics views to link AdWords data to

## Step 4: Choose the Auto-Tagging Settings

Below the Linked View(s) menu shown in Figure 2-2, you will see a statement noting that by linking the AdWords and Google Analytics accounts you will also be enabling auto-tagging for all AdWords accounts in the link groups. You can click on the Advanced Settings links to choose between two options:

- **Enable auto-tagging in any AdWords accounts that were added to the link group (default):** This option appends a unique ID to the end of the destination URL. This ID lets Analytics report the details of each click. Learn more about auto-tagging at `http://goo.gl/9UvX7a`.
- **Leave auto-tagging settings as they are:** For accounts where auto-tagging is disabled, your data will appear as Google organic traffic until you manually add UTMs (refer to Chapter 1, "Implementation Best Practices").

I highly recommend you choose the auto-tagging option, which means AdWords will append a unique ID to destination URLs; this allows Google Analytics to report the details of clicks. It is important to note that if you choose to manually tag your links, you will get less detailed information about your clicks. When you're manually tagging, you have access to only five different dimensions (source, medium, campaign, keyword, and content). However, auto-tagging gives you a much richer set of data, which you will learn more about in the next section.

In addition to having access to more detailed information, you also save the time it would take to tag the links, and you avoid errors coming from the manual process. Last, if you want to import your Google Analytics conversion data and other Google Analytics metrics into your AdWords account, you must use auto-tagging. Learn more about why and how to import Google Analytics goals and transactions into AdWords conversion tracking at `http://goo.gl/kj6nSA`.

Note that when you use auto-tagging, AdWords will append a parameter to your links called `gclid` (which stands for Google Click ID). This parameter has an encoded hashed value that maps back to a specific AdWords click and allows Google Analytics to decode this click ID value and translate it into useful information such as Campaign, AdGroup, Keyword, etc.

But while auto-tagging is more effective and less error-prone, there are special cases where you might not be able to use it. In order to test if auto-tagging will work for your site, follow the instructions at `http://goo.gl/HVvnQR`.

Click Save (see Figure 2-2) and your accounts should now be linked. If you opted to keep auto-tagging turned on, Google Analytics will automatically tag your AdWords links, and you can track the behavior of users coming from your AdWords ads.

## Step 5: Add Brand Terms to Better Classify Your Paid Search Queries

Usually, AdWords search campaigns are composed of two major groups: brand queries, which are those including the name of your company or one of your products, and generic queries, which are those using general queries. The two types of queries often bring customers at a different stage of their buying cycle or with a different knowledge about your company.

- **Brand queries** usually bring customers who have some knowledge about your company; maybe they have even bought from your website in the past. For this reason, you generally expect those queries to have a higher click-through rate (CTR), as the customers apparently know they are looking for you, as well as a low cost per click (CPC). Note that those queries very often see a higher than average percentage of last-click conversions, meaning that the query was the last channel that brought the customer before a conversion; a plausible explanation is that customers searching for a specific brand or product already have made up their minds about what they want to purchase.

- **Generic queries**, on the other hand, often bring a higher than average percentage of new users, with less knowledge about who you are. The CTRs may be lower as customers are not looking specifically for you, and the CPCs may be higher as the competition for generic queries is usually higher. Users coming from generic queries may also be slower to decide on a purchase, as they might still be in the research phase. Therefore, you might see a high number of assisted conversions, meaning that those queries brought users that converted in a later visit to the website.

In the next section, you learn more about naming your AdWords campaigns. You learn that *branded* and *generic* should be part of your campaign names. However, Google Analytics provides a way to better classify your paid search queries by inserting your brand names in the Google Analytics Admin section. This helps you get a more accurate understanding of how brand and generic keywords work together to drive conversions.

Figure 2-3 shows the interface where you add your brand queries. It can be found on the Admin section of your account (log in and click on Admin at the top of your screen). Below your view name you will find a section named Channel Settings. Click on it and then on Manage Brand Terms.

**NOTE**    This is a view-level setting, which means that you should repeat the process for each view you want to include.

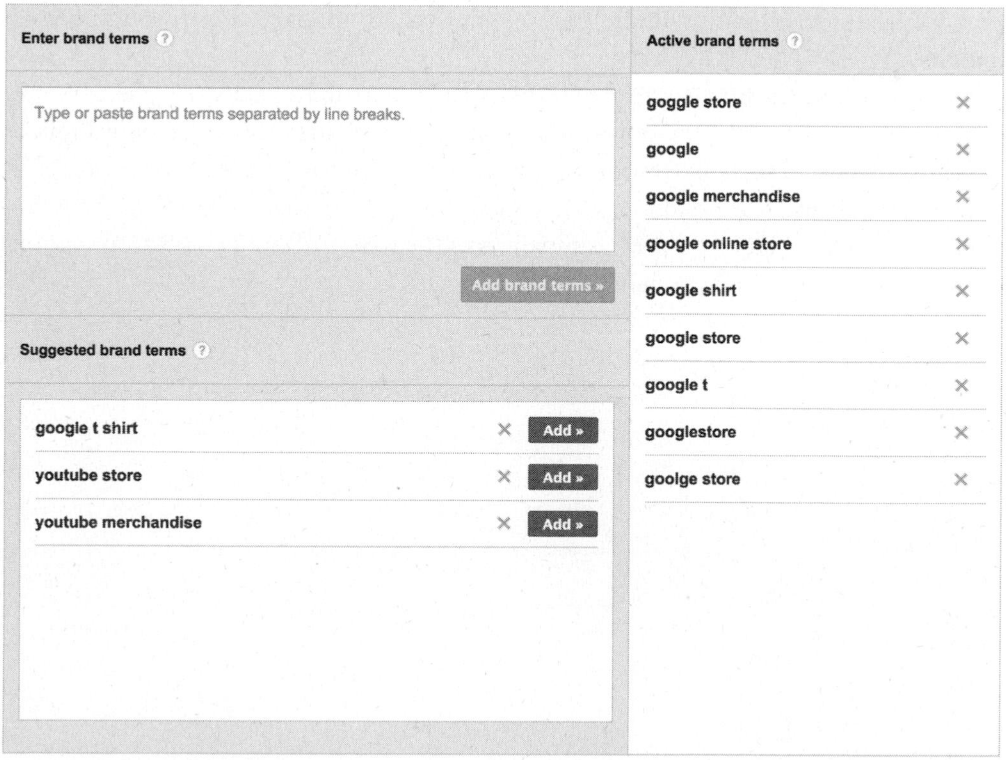

**Figure 2-3:** Adding brand terms to your Channel Settings

When adding brand queries, keep in mind that you do not need to add different variations for plural or capitalization; Google Analytics will include those automatically. However, it is important to think about different misspellings of your company name or products. You might find some ideas in the Queries report in your Webmaster Tools reports inside Google Analytics (read Chapter 5, "Webmaster Tools Integration," for more details).

When you finish adding your brand queries and click Save, you are prompted to create two new channels in the Default Channel grouping, one for brand and one for generic paid search. This will enable you to analyze both types of paid search queries as groups. You can learn about where to find and how to use channel groupings at `http://goo.gl/Jngwhg`.

## Step 6: Create Views for CPC Traffic Only and for Non-CPC Traffic

It is always recommended to have a view in your account with the same settings as your main view, but without AdWords data. This way, you have a backup in case you need to share information with a third party that shouldn't have access to CPC (cost per click) data, also called PPC (pay per click). You should also have a view including only PPC data so that you can share with people who should not have access to all your data but are responsible for managing or reviewing your AdWords campaigns.

Next you learn how to create the filters necessary to set up a view including only Google AdWords traffic. In order to set up a view without Google AdWords, simply change the settings in Figures 2-4 and 2-5 to Exclude instead of Include. To learn more about creating views, visit `http://goo.gl/eevIxD` and to learn more about creating filters, visit `http://goo.gl/T9hjmV`.

The filter in Figure 2-4 will include only CPC campaigns in the view (AdWords with auto-tagging enabled or any manually tagged campaign using `utm_medium=cpc`).

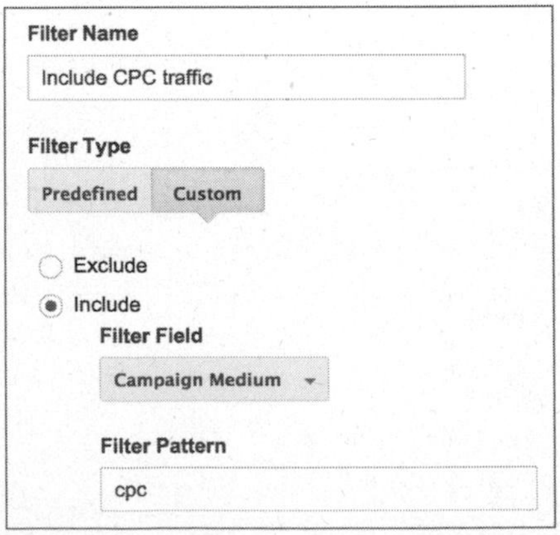

**Figure 2-4:** Filter to include CPC traffic

The filter in Figure 2-5 will include only sessions attributed to Google in the view (either organic or CPC traffic). By adding both filters shown in Figures 2-4 and 2-5 in the same view, you will have only Google CPC campaigns shown in this view.

Note that these views will start collecting data from its creation day. Also note that only tagged sessions attributed to Google CPC will be shown in this view, for example:

- User clicks on tagged AdWords campaign (manual or auto-tagging): *included in the view*.
- User clicks on an AdWords campaign that does not have auto-tagging or manual UTM tags: *not included in the view*.
- User clicks on tagged AdWords campaign, bookmarks the page, and returns a week later directly to website: *included in the view for both sessions*.
- User clicks on tagged AdWords campaign and returns a week later by clicking on an organic search result: *included in the view only on first session*.

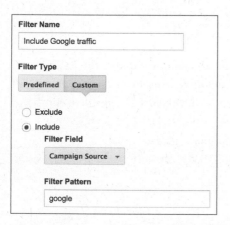

**Figure 2-5:** Filter to include Google traffic

**NOTE**    The preceding examples are not an exhaustive list. For a more comprehensive explanation of how campaign and traffic source data is processed and populated in Google Analytics reports, visit http://goo.gl/4gczFV.

## Deleting and Editing the Google Analytics and AdWords Link

Unlinking Analytics and AdWords accounts from the Google Analytics interface is simple, and the process is the same if you want to manage which views have access to AdWords data. Repeat Steps 1 and 2 and you will find a table similar to the one in Figure 2-6.

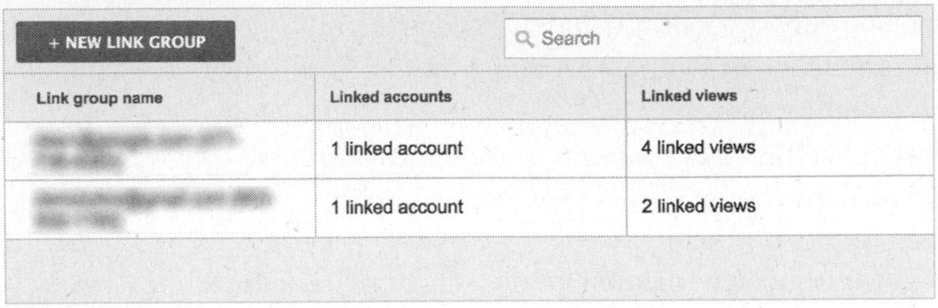

**Figure 2-6:** Deleting and editing Google Analytics and AdWords link

In order to edit or delete a link, click on the Link group name to reach the edit page for it. It will look similar to Figure 2-2.

If you proceed to unlink the accounts, you will receive the following reminder before completing the process:

*If you delete this link group, all data will stop flowing between your AdWords accounts and Analytics property:*

- *AdWords data (i.e., clicks, impressions, CPC, etc.) won't be visible in Analytics reports. Session data up until the time you unlink the account will still be available. Any new sessions that result from clicks in these linked AdWords accounts after you have unlinked will appear in Analytics reports as (not set).*
- *Your Analytics Remarketing Audiences will stop accumulating new users.*
- *AdWords will stop importing all Analytics Goals, ecommerce transactions, and metrics you configured.*

## Top 10 Causes of Google Analytics and AdWords Data Discrepancies

If you followed the previous steps, your data should be accurate. But, if you find numbers that do not match between the tools, it is probably the result of one of the following issues. While other problems might appear, the following Top 10 list covers the vast majority of discrepancies between Google Analytics and AdWords data.

1. The date range being compared includes a period during which the accounts were not linked.
2. There are multiple AdWords accounts linked to the same Google Analytics view, which means data from multiple AdWords accounts is needed in order to match the numbers seen in Google Analytics.

3.  The Google Analytics tracking code is not placed on the ad's landing page, which causes the campaign information to be lost.
4.  There are filters applied to Google Analytics (such as excluding internal IPs, discussed in the first chapter of this book); these filters do not apply to AdWords reports.
5.  Google Analytics and AdWords may not synchronize at the same time, so if the report is very recent (such as same-day reports), the data may not match.
6.  Google AdWords measures clicks, while Google Analytics measures sessions. If a user clicks on an ad twice within 30 minutes without closing the browser, Google Analytics registers one session while AdWords registers two clicks.
7.  AdWords automatically filters invalid clicks (clicks generated by robots or multiple clicks from the same user at the same time), while Google Analytics reports on all the resulting sessions to a website. Note that Google Analytics also has a feature that allows you to exclude bots and spiders (as mentioned in Chapter 1,) but the filtering rules are different from those used by AdWords.
8.  Auto-tagging is turned off and manual tagging was not done correctly.
9.  Cookie expiration dates are different in AdWords and Analytics: AdWords cookies expire 30 days after a customer's click, while Analytics uses a cookie that expires after six months of inactivity. That means if a customer completed a conversion 40 days after clicking on an AdWords ad, the conversion wouldn't be recorded in AdWords but would be recorded in Google Analytics. Note that it is possible to adjust the Google Analytics cookie expiration to match the AdWords cookie expiration; consider doing so cautiously, however, as it might affect other data in Google Analytics. Read more at `http://goo.gl/NiIpos`.
10. If a user comes to your site from an ad, and then leaves the landing page before the tracking code executes, then the `gclid` parameter is never passed to the Google servers and that click is not associated with the session. Alternatively, the landing page may redirect to a different page, which keeps the Google Analytics code from launching on the landing page and properly identifying the session as coming from an AdWords campaign. This might also cause the `gclid` parameter to be lost.

# Integration Data, Structure, and Standard Reports

The integration with AdWords is very valuable for advertisers, as Google Analytics provides robust analysis capabilities concerning AdWords campaigns, allowing marketers to identify how to optimize AdWords spending. In the following sections, you learn what is available once the integration is complete and how you can use the new data to optimize your campaign performance.

## AdWords Dimensions and Metrics in Google Analytics

In order to understand how the different reports in Google Analytics work, you first need to understand the concepts of dimensions and metrics thoroughly. This section contains quick explanations of what dimensions and metrics are, followed by the specific ones that result from the AdWords integration. For a more comprehensive description of dimensions and metrics, visit `http://goo.gl/16JaTU`.

## AdWords Dimensions

Dimensions make up the rows in Google Analytics reports. Google defines a dimension as *a descriptive attribute or characteristic of an object that can be given different values.* In other words, dimensions describe the session, user, product, page, or event. For example, both source and medium are considered dimensions; for a session from an AdWords ad, the source/medium pair will be "`google / cpc`". You can drill down into that dimension to see more granular data (additional dimensions) about the session, such as the ad campaign, the ad keyword, geographic location, browser type, device used, and more.

The following list of AdWords-specific dimensions is available in Google Analytics, in alphabetical order, following the integration. (This is assuming you completed the integration and chose to enable auto-tagging.)

- **Account:** The name of the AdWords account that sent traffic to the website. Each account has a one-to-one ratio with an AdWords customer ID.
- **Ad Content:** The headline of an AdWords ad, which is a useful identifier that is natively set by AdWords in Google Analytics.
- **Ad Distribution Network:** The network where the ad appears. The values can be Google, search partners, or content (display).
- **Ad Group:** As explained in detail in a later section, ad groups make up campaigns and are comprised of keywords, placements, or audiences.
- **Ad Format:** The format of the ad (text, flash, HTML, or image).
- **Ad Slot:** The position of the ad clicked in the search result page, either top or right-hand side (RHS).
- **Ad Slot Position:** The position of the clicked ad within the ad slot. This is assigned 1-3 for top and 1-9 for RHS.
- **Campaign:** As you will see in the next section about AdWords structure, campaign is the highest structural level in an account, where many important targeting settings are set.
- **Campaign Code:** Allows advertisers to automatically set source, medium, and campaign name information based on their own codes.
- **Destination URL:** The full, exact URL entered into the AdWords system that defines the landing page for the ads.
- **Keyword:** The term an advertiser bids on for search campaigns.
- **Keyword Match Type:** Determines how the keyword will trigger (or block) an ad.
- **Matched Search Query:** The exact query that triggered the ad to display.

- **Placement Domain:** The website where a display ad was shown.
- **Placement Type:** Automatic (contextually targeted) or "managed placements" (manually targeted or bid enhanced).
- **Placement URL:** The full exact URL where a display ad was shown, similar to a placement domain, but with more granular data.
- **Query Match Type:** How a keyword was actually matched on Google search. This can differ from the Keyword Match Type.
- **Query Word Count:** Uses a space as the delimiter to provide a count of the words in the search query.
- **Social Annotation Type:** The type of Google Plus annotation made to an ad: none, basic, or personal. Social annotations can display on ads in the Google Display Network.
- **Targeting Type:** How your AdWords ads were targeted: keyword, placement, and vertical targeting.

## AdWords Metrics

Metrics make up the columns in Google Analytics reports; they are the numbers themselves—the actual data. Google defines metrics as the *individual elements of a dimension that can be measured as a sum or a ratio.* A common metric used in multiple Google Analytics reports is "sessions," which is the number of sessions in a certain date range. Other common metrics include bounce rate, pageviews, conversion rate, and revenue.

Metrics offered in the form of a ratio are often calculated by dividing the sum of a particular metric by the number of sessions. For example, the conversion rate for a particular goal is the percentage of sessions when the goal was completed at least once (number of sessions including a goal completion divided by total number of sessions).

This list of AdWords-specific metrics is available on Google Analytics following the integration (shown in alphabetical order).

- **CPC:** Cost per click.
- **CPM:** Cost per 1,000 ad impressions.
- **Clicks:** The total number of clicks received.
- **Cost:** The total cost incurred for clicks and impressions (impressions cost money when doing CPM bidding in the display network).
- **Cost per Conversion:** Cost divided by the sum of ecommerce transactions and goal conversions.
- **Cost per Goal Conversion:** Cost divided by the sum of all goal conversions.
- **Cost per Transaction:** Cost divided by number of ecommerce transactions.
- **CTR:** Click-through rate, which is the ratio of clicks to impressions.
- **Impressions:** The number of times an ad was displayed (or keyword triggered).

- **ROAS:** Return on advertising spend. The (ecommerce revenue + total goal value) divided by cost.
- **RPC:** Return per click. The (ecommerce revenue + total goal value) divided by the clicks.

---

**CURRENCY CONVERSION FROM ADWORDS TO GOOGLE ANALYTICS**

If your Google Analytics View uses a different currency from your AdWords Account, Google Analytics will automatically convert the AdWords cost data to the Google Analytics currency. This AdWords cost data is used in the metrics "Cost," "CPC," and "ROAS" in Google Analytics.

Google Analytics uses the exchange rate at the midpoint of the reporting time range. For example, if you are viewing a time period from January 5th to 19th, the January 12th rate will be used to convert your AdWords cost data to the currency of your Google Analytics account. This conversion makes it easier to compare AdWords cost data to other data in Google Analytics.

---

## AdWords Account Structure Overview

Figure 2-7 shows the hierarchy of an AdWords account. It will serve as a good starting point for understanding AdWords account structure in general and AdWords-specific dimensions in Google Analytics. In this section, you learn about each of the hierarchy levels.

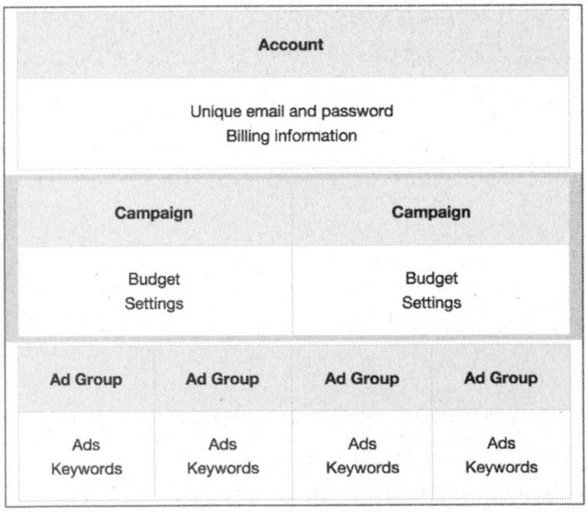

**Figure 2-7:** Google AdWords account structure

## Campaigns

Campaigns are the highest level of an AdWords account. They are particularly important because most targeting and budget settings are controlled at the campaign level.

The following is a list of the most important AdWords campaign settings. For a more comprehensive overview visit `http://goo.gl/aUjVUl`.

- **Campaign Type:** Determines which networks display ads in the campaign. This can be limited to search ads on `google.com` itself, ads on `google.com` and its search partners, shopping campaigns shown on `google.com` (such as product listing ads), or the Google Display Network (GDN), which is the world's largest display advertising network.
- **Shopping Settings:** For shopping campaigns, the inventory of products displayed can be filtered by brand, product type, groupings, or other custom settings as configured in the merchants product feed.
- **Devices:** Determines the bid modifier on computers, smartphones, tablets, or a combination of the three. If an advertiser wants to limit their ads to computers, they would set their mobile and tablet modifier to -100%. Basically, a *bid modifier* alters your base keyword bid in response to predefined signals, such as device, location, day, and time.
- **Location:** Determines the specific geographic location where ads will appear, such as a continent, country, state, city, or particular ZIP code. Bid modifiers can also be set per location.
- **Language:** Limits ad serving to users who have browsers set to the language(s) indicated.
- **Budget:** Specifies the daily budget cap for a campaign.
- **Ad Scheduling:** Establishes days of the week and hours of the day during which ads will display. A bid modifier can be applied to the ad scheduling.
- **Ad Rotation:** Determines how often one ad is chosen to display in relation to other ads within an ad group.

While there are other campaign settings in AdWords, this list contains the settings most relevant to optimizing AdWords performance. Because Google Analytics has dimensions that correspond to network, devices, location, language, and ad scheduling, insights gleaned from Google Analytics data can (and should) directly impact how advertisers configure their campaign settings.

When it comes to naming your campaign, it is important not to use the default campaign names (Campaign #1) or to name the campaign by date of creation (New Campaign Fall 2012). You should always give your campaigns descriptive names that make it easy to determine the focus of the keywords and ads therein. If the campaign is focused on a particular product brand or product type, name it as such. For example, an online food retailer might have one campaign named Sports Drinks and another named Energy Bars. This naming strategy allows the retailer to quickly determine how much money is being spent on each category, and it will also be helpful when analyzing campaign performance. It is also a best practice to have separate campaigns for search and for display advertising.

## Ad Groups

An *ad group* is a set of keywords, ads, and bids; each campaign is made up of one or more ad groups. When a search is performed on `google.com` or a search partner site, the keyword triggered will display one of the ads in the ad group. Ad groups that make up these campaigns should be comprised of tightly knit groupings of keywords that relate very closely to the copy of the ad. Keyword types are discussed in the next subsection.

Ads in the Google Display Network (GDN) can be triggered by a number of different signals, such as keywords, placements, and audiences (including retargeting). When keywords are used in the GDN, the AdWords algorithm contextually places ads within its network. These are known as "automatic placements."

Specific websites can also be added to the ad group and/or bids adjusted for websites discovered through automatic placements. These are known as "managed placements." For example, if you reach the conclusion that the quality of the traffic you get from `online-behavior.com` is particularly relevant, you can bid higher on that particular site to increase the number of times your ad is displayed there.

Google shopping ads are triggered when products uploaded to the Google Merchant Center match a query on Google search. The matching criteria differ from Google search ads, as products are described by a predefined set of fields in the product feed (brand, category, and product type).

Lastly, ads can be targeted to different audiences, which are either groups of websites that are categorically similar or groups of people who have visited your site and have an AdWords remarketing cookie set in their browsers.

## Keywords

In the search network, keywords trigger an ad to display in response to a query. For organic search, a keyword is defined as the exact query that a user entered into the search engine. For pay-per-click (PPC) campaigns, keywords have four match types:

- **Exact Match:** Keyword triggered by the exact query the user searched.
- **Phrase Match:** The query must contain the keyword phrase in the exact order used.
- **Broad Match:** Keyword can also be triggered by conceptually related terms or synonyms; word order does not matter.
- **Modified Broad Match:** Like broad match, but synonyms will not trigger the keyword.

Examples of different matching options can be found at `http://goo.gl/cZATRK`.

# AdWords Standard Reports Overview

Underneath the Acquisition section of the left navigation in Google Analytics, you will find links to all standard reports that Google Analytics offers for AdWords (shown in Figure 2-8). The following is a brief introduction to each of these reports. Methods for using these reports and custom reports to optimize PPC accounts are shared in the next section.

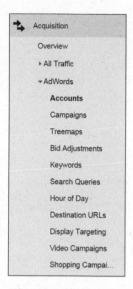

**Figure 2-8:** Google AdWords reports on Google Analytics

## Accounts Report

*The main benefit of this report is that it allows large advertisers to quickly compare the performance of different AdWords accounts.* Some companies use multiple agencies to manage their AdWords campaigns; others have multiple in-house advertising teams, each with their own budget. The Accounts report is designed for companies with these sorts of advertising structures. The direct link to the report is http://goo.gl/oIg8VY. (Note that you will see this report only if you have multiple AdWords accounts linked to your Google Analytics Property.)

Figure 2-9 shows a case where a company has four accounts, one per country. As you can see, the third row, AU (Search), has a significantly lower return on ad spend (ROAS). Evaluating the relative advertising performance of different regions is extremely quick and simple to perform using this report.

Primary Dimension: Account    Campaign    Ad Group

| Account | Sessions | Impressions | Clicks | Cost | CTR | CPC | RPC | ROAS |
|---|---|---|---|---|---|---|---|---|
|  | 2,299,504<br>% of Total: 18.06%<br>(12,732,726) | 119,730,421<br>% of Total: 100.00%<br>(119,730,421) | 2,367,045<br>% of Total: 100.00%<br>(2,367,045) | $742,658.43<br>% of Total: 100.00%<br>($742,658.43) | 1.98%<br>Site Avg: 1.98%<br>(0.00%) | $0.31<br>Site Avg: $0.31<br>(0.00%) | $1.10<br>Site Avg: $5.03<br>(-78.15%) | 350.10%<br>Site Avg: 1,602.02%<br>(-78.15%) |
| 1.   - USA | 1,357,984 (59.06%) | 39,121,417 (32.67%) | 1,226,202 (51.80%) | $434,172.69 (58.46%) | 3.13% | $0.35 | $1.65 | 465.35% |
| 2.   EU | 383,484 (16.68%) | 29,102,949 (24.31%) | 438,684 (18.53%) | $72,705.14 (9.79%) | 1.51% | $0.17 | $0.43 | 260.73% |
| 3.   AU (Search) | 379,223 (16.49%) | 44,730,078 (37.36%) | 496,610 (20.98%) | $182,426.50 (24.56%) | 1.11% | $0.37 | $0.41 | 112.28% |
| 4.   - Canada | 178,813 (7.78%) | 6,775,977 (5.66%) | 205,549 (8.68%) | $53,354.09 (7.18%) | 3.03% | $0.26 | $0.90 | 347.18% |

**Figure 2-9:** Using the Accounts report to evaluate multiple accounts' performance

## Campaigns Report

*The main benefit of this report is that it allows you to quickly identify which campaigns, ad groups, and keywords are performing best and worst.* The Campaigns report allows you to drill down into the different campaigns using the hierarchical structure. As you can see in Figure 2-10, at each level you may choose your table's primary dimension, secondary dimension, metric group, and visualization method. The direct link to the report is `http://goo.gl/Fj45vp`.

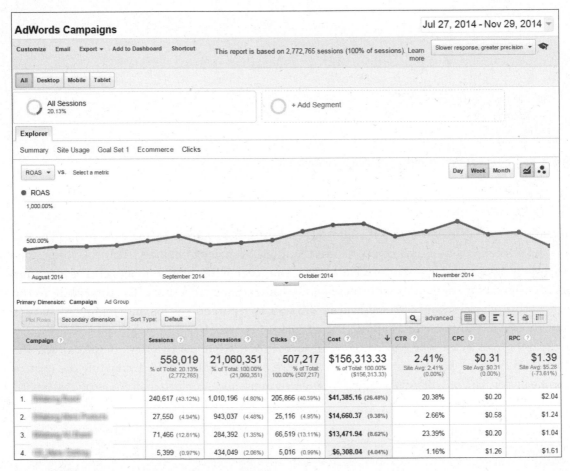

**Figure 2-10:** Campaigns report overview

The drilldown nature of the report allows you to easily see the overall account performance, while at the same time it offers a granularity that can help you gain insights to make pinpoint-level changes.

As with all AdWords standard reports, all of the AdWords-specific metrics are present in the Clicks link on the Metrics group selector (above the line chart in Figure 2-10).

## Treemaps Report

*This report offers a unique data visualization to compare pairs of metrics.* It uses rectangle sizes to represent volume metrics such as clicks, cost, and impressions (the primary metrics). It uses color and saturation to represent relative metrics such as CPC, CTR, and conversion rate (the secondary metrics). Green is positive and red is negative. The darker the green, the better the secondary metric; the darker the red, the worse the secondary metric. The direct link to the report is `http://goo.gl/I6oXMp`.

Figure 2-11 shows an example of an insightful visualization using the Treemaps report. As you can see, the primary metric is cost and the secondary metric is bounce rate (see the drop-down just above the treemap in Figure 2-11). In this example, the advertiser can quickly see which of the brands they are advertising has a high bounce rate in relationship to their spend on those campaigns.

**Figure 2-11:** Visualizing AdWords data with treemaps

Matt Lawson, Director of Performance Ads Marketing for Google, shared three interesting ways to use treemaps in an article following the launch of this feature. Here are the three combinations he shared and how they can help you optimize your AdWords performance:

- **Cost vs. ecommerce conversion rate:** What can you do to increase volume in high converting areas?

■ **Impressions vs. click-through rate:** Which ads are succeeding in turning ad viewers into website visitors?

■ **New users vs. bounce rate:** Which keywords drive new users, and which of those aren't doing a very good job of turning those users into customers?

You can read the full post at `http://goo.gl/SX7M5r`.

## Bid Adjustments Report

AdWords allows you to apply bid modifiers for different devices, geographic locations, and times of day. The Bid Adjustments report shows performance in Google Analytics directly in line with the way that bids are adjusted in AdWords settings. This makes it easy for you to make smart decisions with regard to your bid modifiers. The direct link to this report is `http://goo.gl/TA3NDf`.

While there are other reports in Google Analytics that provide a similar view of ad performance for these dimensions, this particular report is a welcome addition to the advertiser's repertoire. Figure 2-12 shows the report interface; note that you can toggle between bid adjustments settings for device, location, and ad schedule.

| Device | Bid Adj. | Sessions | Impressions | Clicks | Cost | CTR | CPC | RPC | ROAS |
|---|---|---|---|---|---|---|---|---|---|
| | | 22,767 % of Total: 0.68% (3,326,444) | 3,483,434 % of Total: 6.93% (50,260,720) | 20,334 % of Total: 4.58% (443,857) | $5,423.44 % of Total: 1.92% ($282,738.15) | 0.58% Site Avg: 0.88% (-33.90%) | $0.27 Site Avg: $0.64 (-58.13%) | $1.30 Site Avg: $14.18 (-90.86%) | 485.98% Site Avg: 2,225.71% (-78.17%) |
| 1. Mobile devices with full browsers | -15% | 12,865 | 1,620,389 | 11,045 | $2,382.27 | 0.68% | $0.22 | $0.52 | 241.58% |
| 2. Computers | -- | 7,795 | 1,386,140 | 7,438 | $2,243.99 | 0.54% | $0.30 | $2.34 | 776.26% |
| 3. Tablets with full browsers | -- | 2,107 | 476,905 | 1,851 | $797.18 | 0.39% | $0.43 | $1.72 | 399.21% |

**Figure 2-12:** Bid adjustments report on Google Analytics

## Keywords Report

This report is similar to the Campaigns report, but the primary dimensions are keyword and ad content, irrespective of campaign and ad group. *The main benefit of this report is the ability to analyze all keywords in an account in one place, which makes it easy to identify poorly performing keywords across campaigns and ad groups.* It is important to note that the keywords shown in this report are not identifiable by match type unless match type is chosen as a secondary dimension. The direct link to this report is `http://goo.gl/MQsyYq`.

In PPC campaigns, you bid on keywords that are of a particular match type. As such, it is critical to know how a keyword is performing at the match type level. In Figure 2-13, you see a significant difference in performance metrics between the same keyword in phrase match vs. exact match. If you were to look at the keyword report without applying a secondary dimension of match type, you might think that this particular keyword was performing quite well. In reality, the same keyword in phrase match is losing money whereas the exact match is quite profitable.

| | | Keyword | Match Type ⊗ | Visits ↓ | Impressions | Clicks | Cost | CTR | CPC | RPC | ROI |
|---|---|---|---|---|---|---|---|---|---|---|---|
| ☐ | 1. | | Phrase match | **1,230** | 13,757 | 1,207 | $2,055.66 | 8.77% | $1.70 | $0.84 | -50.81% |
| ☐ | 2. | | Exact match | 510 | 1,822 | 429 | $245.95 | 23.55% | $0.57 | $27.04 | 4,616.89% |

**Figure 2-13:** Keywords report segmented by match type

## Search Queries Report

*The Search Queries report is extremely useful for both keyword research and finding opportunities to add negative keywords to your AdWords campaigns.* The report defaults to two primary dimensions: matched search query and match type. The direct link to this report is `http://goo.gl/f9Wdpr`.

From a keyword research perspective, having the full list of queries that brought people to your site can help identify well performing search terms that you might not be currently bidding on. On the flip side, there are times when broad and phrase match keywords bring non-relevant traffic to your site. Using this report, you can quickly browse through the actual search queries to add to negative keyword lists. A step-by-step guide to using matched search queries for adding negative keywords follows in the optimization section of this chapter.

Currently, the match search queries dimension is not mapped to AdWords cost data metrics. In order to view information such as total spend or cost per click for these queries, use the Keyword Details report underneath the Keywords tab in the AdWords interface.

Also note that you might find a "(not set)" entry on the matched search queries report. In most cases, this is traffic from the Google Display Network where there indeed was no query performed. Other reasons "(not set)" can occur include mobile browsers not passing referrer information to Google Analytics or searches being conducted on a Google encrypted search.

## Hour of Day Report

The Hour of Day report enables you to explore hour-of-day and day-of-week dimensions. *This report is useful for gaining insights into optimizing ad scheduling in campaign settings within AdWords.* The direct link to the report is `http://goo.gl/2aHftq`.

In Figure 2-14 you can see two lines: a darker line representing the metric *Per Session Value* and a lighter line representing the total sessions. Both are shown on an hourly basis. The chart shows very clearly that while traffic (sessions) peaks between 5 and 8 PM, the *Per Session Value* of users is highest during the morning hours, between 6 and 9 AM. When you visit the default report (link in previous paragraph), the Sessions metric will show by default, with only one line in the chart; to create a similar chart, add a second line by clicking in the drop-down in the upper-left corner of the line chart in Figure 2-14.

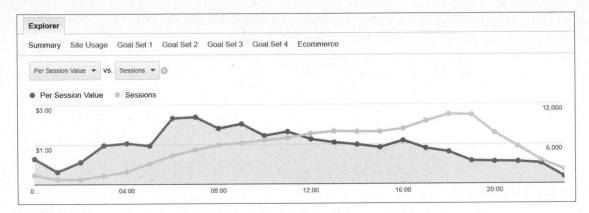

**Figure 2-14:** Line chart comparing sessions and value per hour

Another useful way to analyze the Hour of Day and Day of Week Name dimensions is to export the data from Google Analytics into a spreadsheet and apply conditional formatting to it, as shown in Figure 2-15.

| Sum of Conv Rate | Column Labels | | | | | | |
|---|---|---|---|---|---|---|---|
| Hour | Sunday | Monday | Tuesday | Wednesday | Thursday | Friday | Saturday |
| 0 | 1.95% | 1.63% | 3.16% | 1.38% | 1.15% | 1.62% | 1.20% |
| 1 | 0.97% | 2.06% | 1.06% | 0.86% | 1.59% | 0.61% | 0.96% |
| 2 | 1.90% | 1.95% | 2.70% | 1.11% | 0.78% | 1.44% | 1.07% |
| 3 | 1.24% | 1.80% | 2.11% | 0.00% | 0.98% | 0.55% | 2.58% |
| 4 | 0.74% | 2.49% | 2.58% | 0.00% | 1.90% | 1.52% | 1.52% |
| 5 | 0.88% | 3.55% | 3.17% | 2.03% | 0.93% | 1.27% | 2.09% |
| 6 | 1.94% | 5.19% | 1.82% | 1.56% | 2.26% | 3.72% | 1.69% |
| 7 | 1.34% | 3.55% | 2.32% | 1.21% | 2.05% | 3.11% | 2.23% |
| 8 | 1.01% | 4.03% | 2.28% | 1.93% | 2.05% | 2.37% | 2.57% |
| 9 | 2.38% | 4.57% | 2.91% | 2.29% | 1.39% | 2.72% | 1.18% |
| 10 | 1.66% | 3.25% | 2.40% | 2.16% | 1.90% | 2.72% | 2.17% |
| 11 | 2.52% | 4.19% | 2.57% | 2.49% | 1.48% | 2.14% | 1.87% |
| 12 | 1.48% | 3.48% | 1.95% | 1.59% | 1.85% | 3.29% | 2.32% |
| 13 | 2.04% | 3.06% | 2.32% | 2.55% | 1.81% | 1.87% | 1.94% |
| 14 | 2.07% | 2.70% | 1.96% | 1.88% | 1.77% | 2.15% | 1.95% |
| 15 | 2.41% | 2.83% | 1.95% | 1.60% | 1.61% | 2.93% | 2.28% |
| 16 | 1.89% | 2.87% | 1.76% | 1.63% | 1.58% | 2.00% | 1.54% |
| 17 | 1.40% | 2.63% | 1.77% | 1.55% | 1.94% | 2.14% | 2.19% |
| 18 | 2.45% | 3.22% | 1.99% | 1.10% | 1.27% | 2.63% | 1.80% |
| 19 | 2.60% | 3.90% | 2.10% | 1.32% | 1.67% | 1.99% | 1.84% |
| 20 | 2.25% | 3.45% | 1.43% | 1.44% | 1.62% | 1.63% | 1.60% |
| 21 | 1.73% | 3.74% | 1.61% | 1.67% | 1.38% | 1.14% | 1.56% |
| 22 | 1.72% | 3.82% | 1.46% | 1.55% | 1.75% | 1.72% | 1.59% |
| 23 | 2.05% | 1.82% | 1.69% | 1.06% | 0.86% | 0.92% | 1.28% |
| Grand Total | 1.97% | 3.35% | 2.03% | 1.67% | 1.62% | 2.17% | 1.83% |

**Figure 2-15:** Hour of Day and Day of Week Name exported

If you were responsible for the campaign shown in Figure 2-15, you would be well advised to adjust the ad scheduling settings in the campaigns to drive more traffic to the site on Mondays and Friday mornings, as that traffic is more likely to convert.

The following steps are required to change the ad scheduling on the AdWords interface:

1. Navigate to a specific campaign in the AdWords interface.
2. Choose the Campaign Settings tab.
3. Under Advanced Settings, click the plus (+) box next to Schedule: Start Date, End Date, Ad Scheduling.
4. Next to Ad Scheduling, choose Edit.
5. Edit the times you want your ads to appear or periods that you want to adjust.
6. Click View Ad Schedule to see your scheduling and add a bid modifier.
7. Adjust the bid settings (using a percent multiplier to increase or decrease bids).
8. Click Save.

## Destination URLs Report

The Destination URLs report is designed to explore your destination URLs, but it also allows you to analyze your ad distribution networks and keywords by changing the primary dimension through the selector above the table. Note that destination URLs are the pages defined on AdWords as the destinations that users will be sent to when clicking on your ads. The direct link to this report is `http://goo.gl/n1k6df`.

When a new user clicks on one of your ads for the first time, the Destination URL is the same as the Landing Page. However, if this same user saves one of your pages as a bookmark and returns at a later date, he may land in a different page, but his visit will still be attributed to the same campaign and Destination URL; in such cases this report will show the original Destination URL for the campaign, not the actual Landing Page. At the time of this writing, the landing page dimension is not available in any of the standard AdWords reports, so you must rely on Destination URL report (or use Custom Reports). Note that Destination URLs cannot be rewritten with filters in Google Analytics; they will always appear as configured in AdWords campaigns.

The destination URL is an excellent way to add tracking parameters that distinguish between ads. The ad content dimension in Google Analytics AdWords reports, while useful, will only provide the headline for ads. When two different ads share the same headline but split testing is being performed on the rest of the ad copy, there is no default way for Google Analytics to report which ad was clicked by the user. Adding a tracking parameter to the destination URL in AdWords is a great way to gain visibility into ad split testing. This tracking parameter can be removed from all other reports via Google Analytics view settings, but will remain in the destination URL of AdWords reports.

Note that destination URLs are displayed as "not set" for shopping campaign traffic.

## Display Targeting Report

The Display Targeting report provides quick access to reporting on the main ways that users can be targeted on the Google Display Network: display keywords, placements, topics, interests and remarketing, age, and gender. Figure 2-16 shows a standard Display Targeting report. Note that above the table is an extra selector where you can choose between the different targeting options.

| | Display Keywords | Placements | Topics | Interests and Remarketing | Age | Gender | | | | | |
|---|---|---|---|---|---|---|---|---|---|---|---|

| Secondary dimension | Sort Type: Default |

| **Placements** | Acquisition | | | | Behavior | | | Conversions eCommerce ▾ | |
|---|---|---|---|---|---|---|---|---|---|
| | Clicks ? ↓ | Cost ? | CPC ? | Sessions ? | Bounce Rate ? | Pages / Session ? | Transactions ? | Revenue ? |
| | **9,309**<br>% of Total:<br>2.97% (313,300) | **$4,746.33**<br>% of Total: 3.49%<br>($135,981.15) | **$0.51**<br>Site Avg:<br>$0.43<br>(17.47%) | **11,436**<br>% of Total: 1.74%<br>(655,921) | **61.13%**<br>Site Avg:<br>60.22%<br>(1.52%) | **3.91**<br>Site Avg:<br>3.57 (9.50%) | **119**<br>% of Total: 0.84%<br>(14,097) | **$26,022.91**<br>% of Total: 1.01%<br>($2,567,512.61) |
| Automatic placements | 9,309(100.00%) | $4,746.33(100.00%) | $0.51 | 11,436(100.00%) | 61.13% | 3.91 | 119(100.00%) | $26,022.91(100.00%) |

**Figure 2-16:** Display Targeting options selector

You can set these targeting options in AdWords directly in the Display Network tab in a campaign. Selecting the red + Targeting button will open an interface for choosing audience segments to target.

The data within the Display Targeting report is for traffic that was already targeted in AdWords. To provide advertisers with greater visibility into how different targets behave on websites, Google offers the Display Advertising integration with Google Analytics. This integration will associate the DoubleClick cookie with sessions in Google Analytics. By having this integration enabled, advertisers can view how users in different demographic and interest categories behave on their site. This data is *highly actionable,* as site owners can choose to target audiences that have a high likelihood of conversion and exclude audiences from display advertising that do not convert well. Learn how to enable this feature at `http://goo.gl/Cu88r6`.

Google Analytics has a set of native reports under Audience > Demographics (the direct link to the report is `http://goo.gl/xGAOBD`) where this data can be accessed. The simplest way to take action on this data is to look at the conversion rates for different audiences and demographics and then adjust bids/targeting accordingly.

Figure 2-17 shows a visualization that can be extremely insightful when it comes to understanding your audiences and finding ways to fine-tune your targeting using Google Analytics data. The figure shows different age groups (first column) and is sorted by average order value (second column); the third column (with the bars) shows, for each age group, how it compares to the website average when it comes to ecommerce conversion rate. In this case, you might decide to invest more heavily on users between 45 and 54 years old, as they have a high average order value and ecommerce conversion rate.

In the same way you can analyze performance by age groups, you can also analyze performance by gender, affinity categories, in-market segments, and other categories. You can find a quick overview with some optimization ideas at `http://goo.gl/PPwe8X`.

Direct performance of interest-based audience lists and remarketing lists can be seen in the Interests and Remarketing tab inside the Display Targeting report, as shown in Figure 2-18. Note that all remarketing lists in your AdWords account will show here, not just those lists created in

Google Analytics. The next section has a full discussion of how to create remarketing lists for the display network using custom segments.

**Figure 2-17:** Optimizing targeting using demographic data

| Interests and Remarketing | Sessions | Impressions | Clicks | Cost | CTR | CPC | RPC | ROAS |
|---|---|---|---|---|---|---|---|---|
| | 22,378 % of Total: 1.26% (1,776,156) | 6,683,176 % of Total: 22.97% (29,095,431) | 23,719 % of Total: 4.88% (485,676) | $23,391.51 % of Total: 2.48% ($943,266.90) | 0.35% Site Avg: 1.67% (-78.74%) | $0.99 Site Avg: $1.94 (-49.22%) | $0.65 Site Avg: $15.29 (-95.78%) | 65.45% Site Avg: 787.24% (-91.69%) |
| 1. Past buyers | 435 (1.94%) | 128,735 (1.93%) | 417 (1.76%) | $535.87 (2.29%) | 0.32% | $1.29 | $4.48 | 348.87% |
| 2. Shopping cart abandoners | 679 (3.03%) | 122,758 (1.84%) | 649 (2.74%) | $761.40 (3.26%) | 0.53% | $1.17 | $3.53 | 301.10% |
| 3. Product viewers | 9,983 (44.61%) | 1,953,080 (29.22%) | 10,408 (43.88%) | $10,706.84 (45.77%) | 0.53% | $1.03 | $0.75 | 73.28% |
| 4. All Site Visitors | 5,261 (23.51%) | 2,970,869 (44.45%) | 5,806 (24.48%) | $3,459.65 (14.79%) | 0.20% | $0.60 | $0.32 | 54.21% |

**Figure 2-18:** Interests and Remarketing tab

## Video Campaigns Report

The Video Campaigns report provides rich data on the performance of ads on YouTube. Special video campaign metrics are broken down into website clicks and engagement data. The direct link to the report is http://goo.gl/e2zOTx.

The additional metrics available in this report include:

- **Impressions:** The number of times the ad was shown.
- **Paid Views:** The number of times the TrueView ad was viewed.

- **Website Clicks:** Clicks to the advertiser's website, YouTube channel, or other sites.
- **Cost:** Total cost of the campaign.
- **Website CTR:** Number of clicks divided by paid views.
- **CPV:** Cost per view.
- **Earned Views:** Number of views from users who watched a paid ad and then viewed other videos in the advertiser's YouTube account.
- **Earned Subscribers:** Users who subscribe after viewing an ad.
- **Video Played to XX%:** Indication of engagement with the video.

## Shopping Campaigns Report

Shopping campaigns are special campaigns that house Product Listing Ads (PLAs). PLAs, such as the example shown in the top-right side of Figure 2-19, are unique ad formats that allow you to include an image, title, price, promotional message, and your store or business name, without having to create unique ads for each product you sell.

PLAs show within the Google shopping search results or on `google.com` (for relevant queries). At the time of publication, Google shopping is currently available in the United States, the United Kingdom, Australia, Germany, France, Japan, Italy, the Netherlands, Brazil, Spain, Switzerland, and the Czech Republic. The direct link to the report is `http://goo.gl/rrrzPc`.

In order to advertise using PLAs, you need to have a Google Merchant Account where you can upload your product data feed. The product data feed, a structured list of your merchandise, needs to match a particular format. For more information about how to get started with the Merchant Center, see `http://goo.gl/WiRtUV`.

The Shopping Campaigns report in Google Analytics provides advertisers with three unique dimensions to explore PLA performance (see the top of Figure 2-20):

- **Shopping Category:** Product groupings according to Google's product taxonomy.
- **Shopping Product Type:** Product groupings according to the merchant's own product taxonomy.
- **Shopping Brand:** The brand of the product.

While shopping campaigns do not target keywords, as in search campaigns, you will see a "keyword" associated with clicks, namely, the product_type and custom fields associated with the product in the feed. Keep this in mind when looking at the Keywords report or other reports where you set a keyword as a dimension. In a similar vein, Google Analytics will show a matched search query dimension for queries that led to clicks on shopping campaigns. This is a very useful way to add negative keywords to campaigns as a method for suppressing PLA impressions for irrelevant or poorly converting queries.

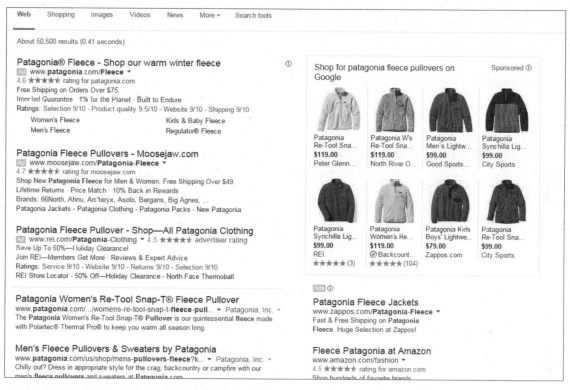

**Figure 2-19:** Product Listing Ads on Google Search

| | Campaign | Acquisition | | | |
|---|---|---|---|---|---|
| | | Clicks ↓ | Cost | CPC | Sessions |
| | | 276,977<br>% of Total: 78.00%<br>(355,076) | $109,120.16<br>% of Total: 69.83%<br>($156,259.33) | $0.39<br>Site Avg: $0.44<br>(-10.48%) | 290,081<br>% of Total: 39.54%<br>(733,717) |
| ☐ | 1. Shopping | 276,977 (100.00%) | $109,120.16 (100.00%) | $0.39 | 290,078 (100.00%) |

Primary Dimension: **Campaign**   Shopping Category Level 1   Shopping Product Type Level 1   Shopping Brand

Plot Rows   Secondary dimension ▼   Sort Type: Default ▼

**Figure 2-20:** Shopping campaigns report dimensions

# Optimizing AdWords Performance Using Google Analytics

This section is a guide to optimizing AdWords performance based on the integration discussed in this chapter. In this section, you learn beginner, intermediate, and advanced PPC skillsets with insights into how to access the valuable data that Google Analytics has to offer to PPC optimizers and analysts.

## Identifying Winners and Losers—The ABC Framework

When thinking about measuring the performance of inbound traffic in Google Analytics, Avinash Kaushik provides a highly insightful framework: Acquisition, Behavior, and Outcomes (known in the Google Analytics interface as the ABCs—Acquisition, Behavior, and Conversions). You can read Avinash's post for a full description of his proposed framework at http://goo.gl/OWjW7x.

The ABCs are a way to group different metrics. Acquisition metrics measure the number of people coming to the website, the percentage of new users, the cost to acquire them, and others. Behavior metrics measure the interaction of users with the website apart from goals: bounce rate, pages per session, time spent on site, and others. Conversion metrics measure the desired actions that users take on the site, such as conversion rates, per visit value, ROI, and others.

While the standard AdWords reports described in the previous section are extremely useful, ultimately using Custom Reports will provide more flexibility in the analysis and allow you to put most of your key performance indicators (KPIs) on the same screen without the need to flip between tabs. For example, Bounce Rate and Per Session Value can be in the same tab, even though they are usually separated, the former being under the Site Usage metric group and the latter under the Ecommerce metric group.

Figure 2-21 shows a custom report configuration, which includes a mapping of each metric to the ABC framework. The example is for an ecommerce store; you can create this custom report by logging into your account and opening the following link: http://goo.gl/5WDvbD.

Following the creation of the custom report, you will be able to sort, filter, and segment the data to determine which campaigns (or ad groups or keywords) should be paused, which bids should be adjusted, and which campaign settings should be changed.

A good starting point for identifying winners and losers is the bounce rate metric. While bounce rate definitely needs to be analyzed contextually, in most circumstances advertisers bring visitors to their websites hoping that the visitor has some level of interaction with it (such as browsing multiple products, downloading a white paper, or filling out a contact form). For most PPC accounts, a high bounce rate is problematic. For a more detailed analysis of how to interpret bounce rates, read http://goo.gl/FsEQ4p.

However, simply sorting the list of campaigns by bounce rate from high to low shows a number of irrelevant campaigns due to very low traffic. Instead, you should apply weighted sort to the bounce rate column. Google Analytics will then automatically sort the list of campaigns by weighted importance (see how to perform this in Figure 2-22). All the campaigns that float to the top deserve drilling down into their ad groups and keywords to analyze if any of them is leading to wasteful spending.

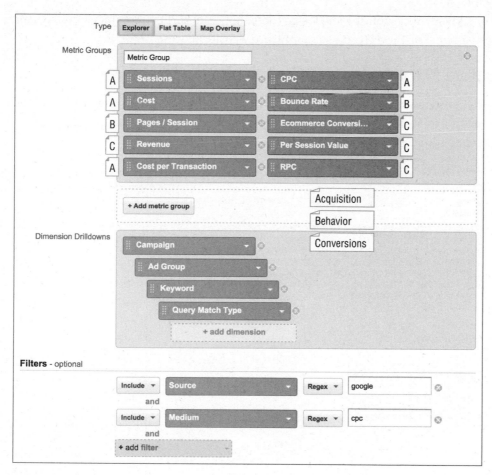

**Figure 2-21:** AdWords custom report mapped to ABC framework

Primary Dimension: Campaign    **Ad Group**

| | Plot Rows | Secondary dimension ▾ | Sort Type: | Default ▾ | | | |

| | | | Default | | | **Behavior** |
|---|---|---|---|---|---|---|
| | | | Absolute Change | | | |
| | **Ad Group** ⑦ | | Weighted | | | |
| | | Sessions ⑦ | Sessions ⑦ | New Users ⑦ | | Bounce Rate ⑦ ↓ |
| | | 17,379 % of Total: 32.87% (52,867) | 68.86% Avg for View: 73.37% (-6.14%) | 11,967 % of Total: 30.85% (38,786) | | 80.87% Avg for View: 42.25% (91.41%) |
| ☐ | 1.  Integrations Display | 17,374 (99.97%) | 68.87% | 11,966 (99.99%) | | **80.87%** |

**Figure 2-22:** Using weighted sort helps the analysis be more relevant

Another way to quickly identify winning and losing campaigns is to sort by ecommerce conversion rate or goal conversion rate, whichever you use to measure website success.

## Finding Negative Keywords with Custom Reports

Figure 2-23 shows the configuration for a custom report that can be used to identify opportunities for adding negative keywords to ad groups or campaigns. You can create this custom report by logging into your account and opening the following link: `http://goo.gl/y4kfx3`.

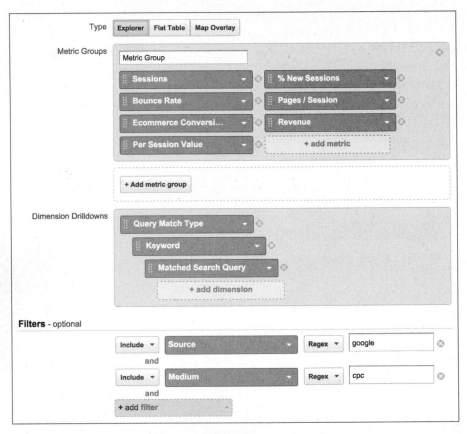

**Figure 2-23:** Custom report to assist finding negative keywords

The first level of drill down is the match type. Since the objective is to find search queries that aren't relevant to the website, it's better to drill down into either broad or phrase match.

Drilling down from the keyword into the matched search query dimension reveals the culprits of the high bounce rate. If, for example, a particular advertiser sells the Hickory brand of cabinet hardware, yet matches on queries specifically for "tools handles" or "axe handles," adding them as negative keywords can save money and improve profitability.

# Creating Remarketing Lists Using Google Analytics Data

One of the most powerful components of the Display & Interests integration is the ability to create remarketing lists *directly from Google Analytics*. According to Google (`http://goo.gl/rNbL2k`):

> *Remarketing with Google Analytics lets you deliver targeted ads to users who have already been to your site and you can base those ads on behavior those users displayed during their sessions.*

Creating remarketing lists from inside Google Analytics can be accomplished by building audiences directly from the Segment Builder. Segments, which can be created from any valid dimension/metric combination, allow you to see how subsets of users behave on your site in comparison to all users or to another subset. In other words, segments allow you to see things such as all sessions where a particular action was taken or all users who meet a particular criteria.

**NOTE**   In order to use Remarketing on Google Analytics, you need to Enable Display Advertising, as explained in Chapter 1. You can also find the full implementation details at `http://goo.gl/2FOKNS`.

For example, you may want to remarket to users who have added an item to their cart but have not purchased. To do so, you would follow these steps:

1. Create a segment for all users who viewed their shopping cart but did not make a purchase, as shown in Figure 2-24 (note that this segment assumes that you have a goal that triggers every time users view a shopping cart).

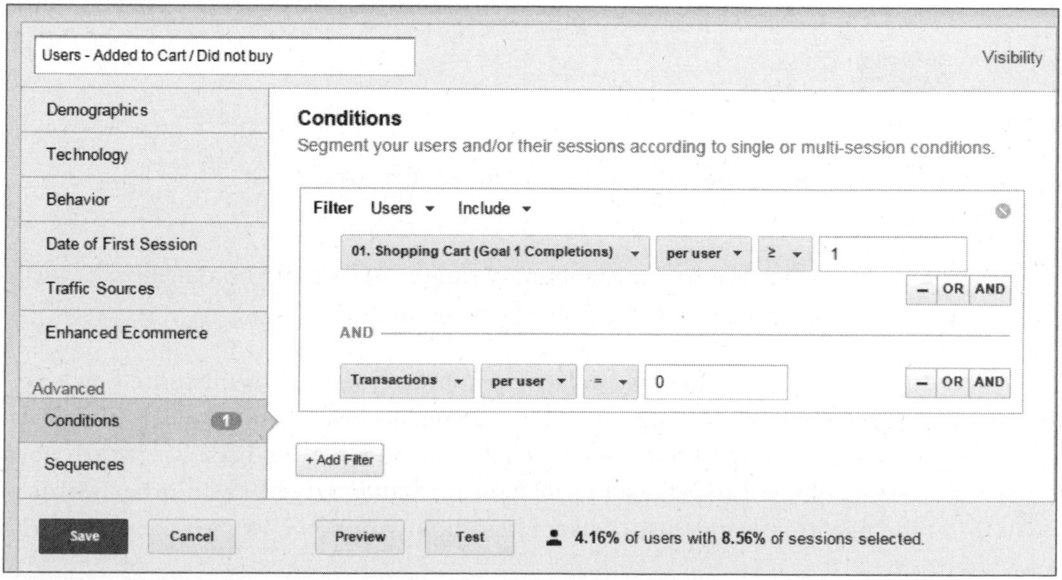

**Figure 2-24:** Creating a segment for users who viewed the shopping cart

2. After the segment is saved, click the down arrow on the segment, as shown in Figure 2-25, and select Build Audience.

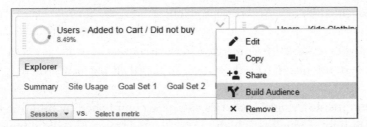

**Figure 2-25:** Building an audience based on a Google Analytics segment

3. You will be immediately directed to the Google Analytics admin section, where you should select in which AdWords account to store the audience list (see Figure 2-26).

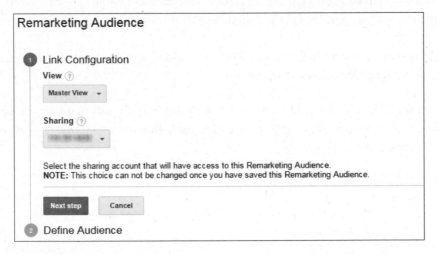

**Figure 2-26:** Choosing the AdWords account to save the audience list

4. Select a lookback window and the amount of time a user should be a member of the list, give the audience a name, and then click Save (see Figure 2-27).

The preceding step-by-step guide is a relatively simple case used to illustrate how easy it is to create remarketing audiences using segments. Since segments leverage *all available* Google Analytics data, you can engender powerful business logic for your remarketing lists. It is worth noting that audience lists in AdWords can be used to *include or exclude* targeting. In other words, Google Analytics can be used to create a list of users for whom you do *not* want to see your ads on the display network.

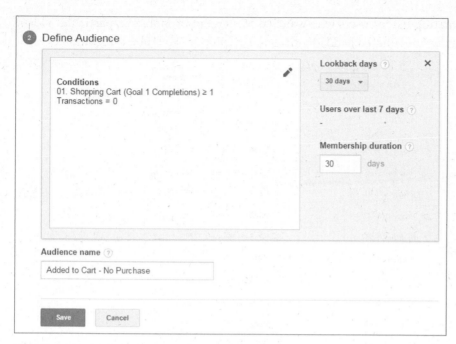

**Figure 2-27:** Defining the audience list settings

Here are a few more examples of how Google Analytics can leverage business logic to build audience lists.

## Remarketing for Ecommerce Business

For retailers using Enhanced Ecommerce reporting, a full view of consumer interaction with their merchandise can be seen in Google Analytics. Common ecommerce actions, such as viewing a product, adding to cart, checking out, and purchasing are visible at all levels of product taxonomy (hierarchy). Such tracking allows Google Analytics to calculate metrics such as a "buy to detail rate," or how often a product is purchased in relationship to how often it is viewed.

Knowing which product categories had a high propensity for purchase vs. a lower propensity for purchase can create powerful remarketing lists. Similarly, if a retailer knows that a certain product or product type was purchased, highly relevant ads targeting upsells and cross-sells can be served.

## Remarketing for B2B and SaaS Business

For B2B or SaaS businesses, oftentimes a value proposition is presented via video. Knowing whether a user has heard that value proposition can make a big difference in terms of how to target that user with further advertising. In Figure 2-28 you can see an example of an implementation that includes specific video behavior, including the percentage watched. Based on this information, you might choose to create a remarketing list for users who watched 50 percent or more of a particular video. Read more about measuring YouTube-embedded videos in Chapter 6, "YouTube Integration."

| | Event Category | Event Action | Total Events ↓ | Unique Events |
|---|---|---|---|---|
| | | | **11,385** % of Total: 24.19% (47,068) | **6,443** % of Total: 34.03% (18,932) |
| ☐ | 1. Video | Progress %10 | **1,504** (13.21%) | 833 (12.93%) |
| ☐ | 2. Video | Progress %20 | **1,414** (12.42%) | 787 (12.21%) |
| ☐ | 3. Video | Progress %30 | **1,359** (11.94%) | 762 (11.83%) |
| ☐ | 4. Video | Progress %40 | **1,302** (11.44%) | 736 (11.42%) |
| ☐ | 5. Video | Progress %50 | **1,262** (11.08%) | 715 (11.10%) |
| ☐ | 6. Video | Progress %60 | **1,216** (10.68%) | 692 (10.74%) |
| ☐ | 7. Video | Progress %70 | **1,165** (10.23%) | 672 (10.43%) |
| ☐ | 8. Video | Progress %80 | **1,121** (9.85%) | 647 (10.04%) |
| ☐ | 9. Video | Progress %90 | **1,042** (9.15%) | 599 (9.30%) |

**Figure 2-28:** Define audience list settings

As mentioned previously, all data collected in Google Analytics can be used to create audience lists for the display network. In addition to the previous example, you can add rules to remarket to users who have viewed at least half of a particular video but did not register for the site.

In another SaaS example, a business may want to target registered users who have not visited their site recently to use their product. In this way, they can give these prospective customers a "reminder" message on the display network while limiting ad impressions to people who are already active users of a free trial.

## Optimizing Shopping Campaigns

Generally speaking, you can optimize shopping campaigns by bidding strongly on product groupings that convert well. In addition, you can decrease bids on weaker performing products or suppress those products from the Merchant Center's data feed altogether.

As mentioned earlier, the Shopping Campaigns report allows you to drill into product performance according to a merchandising taxonomy or by brand. Similar product performance reports are part of Google Analytics in a section of reporting known as Enhanced Ecommerce. The Enhanced Ecommerce reports are a full suite of reporting that helps retailers measure their sales funnel (shopping progression and abandonment), product performance, and certain marketing activities such as internal promotions, order coupons, product discounts, or affiliate sales. The product performance reports in particular give advertisers useful data to make decisions about how to manage their shopping campaigns. Read more about Enhanced Ecommerce at `http://goo.gl/uphWdz`.

Figure 2-29 shows a series of dimensions and metrics that can uncover users' propensity for product purchase as you drill down into the product taxonomy. It is highly recommended for your product categorization in your Merchant Center data feed to match the categorization you pass to Enhanced Ecommerce reports. Knowing which products are likely/unlikely to be purchased when viewed will guide bidding strategy and inclusion of products in the Merchant Center.

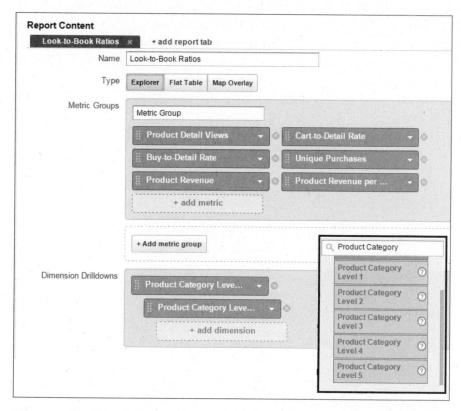

**Figure 2-29:** Shopping campaign performance metrics

# Summary

As you have learned in this chapter, integrating AdWords is a quick and smooth process, and managing linked accounts is very simple. You also learned about discrepancies when it comes to Google Analytics and AdWords data and read a Top 10 list of issues that might cause them.

Once the integration is completed, you will have a powerful tool to optimize AdWords campaigns. Basically, the advantage of using Google Analytics along with AdWords for campaign performance analysis is that it enables you to link AdWords data to overall website usage in a synergetic way. Here are some of the tips that you learned in this chapter:

- Create separate views for both CPC and non-CPC traffic, as this will be helpful for controlling access to Google Analytics and AdWords data as well as for performing advanced analysis.
- Add your brand names in your Google Analytics settings to get a more accurate understanding of how brand and generic keywords work together to drive conversions.
- Create remarketing lists using Google Analytics to reach your most relevant potential customers.
- Adjust the ad scheduling settings in your AdWords campaigns to drive more traffic during hours when traffic is more valuable.
- Use Custom Reports wisely in order to understand more effectively how your campaigns are performing.
- Use Google Analytics to find negative keywords that should be removed from your AdWords campaigns.

# 3

# AdSense Integration

Content publishers have an important role on the web: They make information available to the world so that people know what is happening at any given time and place. They can take the form of large news portals, personal blogs, or anything in between, and they have different ways to monetize content—advertising, subscriptions, premium content, and others. Among the publishers that monetize their content through advertising, both small and big, there is a large number who use AdSense, a solution offered by Google to serve text, image, video, or other advertisements that are targeted to a site's content and its audience.

Because AdSense is so important to so many users, the Google Analytics team developed an integration between the tools that provide a wealth of information about the performance of ads served in a website, along with other behavioral data. This integration helps publishers understand the behavior of their readers by identifying which traffic sources, geographies, pages, and other segments bring the highest-value users to their websites. It empowers publishers to understand who clicks (or not) on an ad, enabling a data-driven approach to optimizing content for AdSense revenue.

In this chapter, you learn how to link AdSense accounts to Google Analytics properties and how to analyze the reports that come with the integration. You also learn tips for advanced analyses of AdSense performance using Google Analytics standard features.

## Integrating AdSense and Google Analytics

In this section, you learn about the process of linking, unlinking, and managing access to AdSense data within Google Analytics. Next, you learn what can potentially cause data discrepancies between the stats returned from each tool.

### Linking Analytics to AdSense

Before you link the accounts, it is important to understand what will and what will not be seen in your Google Analytics reports. Google Analytics shows clicks, impressions, and earnings for ad units shown through AdSense for content. However, it will not show link units, search boxes, mobile ads, or any other AdSense product.

## Step 1: Make Sure You Have the Necessary Access Levels

When it comes to user access, the integration can be accomplished only if you have Edit rights on Google Analytics and are an Administrator on AdSense. Here are links to the relevant Help Center articles for information on how to grant the right access levels:

- Google Analytics: `http://goo.gl/bxyNkC`
- AdSense: `http://goo.gl/J1QBSO`

## Step 2: Find the Product Linking Section

In order to link your Google Analytics and AdSense, log in to your Google Analytics account and click Admin at the top of your screen. Then, choose the property you want to link to your AdSense account and look for a menu item named AdSense Linking or All Products.

**NOTE** The linking happens at the property level, but as you will learn, you can still make the data available on a view basis.

If you have no AdSense accounts linked, you will see a table similar to Figure 3-1.

**Figure 3-1:** AdSense linking table

## Step 3: Choose the AdSense Account You Want to Link

Click on the + New AdSense Link button (top-left of the table in Figure 3-1) in order to start the linking process. You will see a list of all the AdSense accounts you are the Administrator for. Check which AdSense Publisher ID you would like to link to and then click on the radio button to choose which AdSense property from that account you want to link to. In Figure 3-2, you can see a Google Analytics user with access to only one publisher ID (`pub-5054206726270162`) and one AdSense product (AdSense for Content).

## Step 4: Choose Which Google Analytics Views Will Report AdSense Data

After you choose the AdSense account and property to be linked to, you will be asked which views should include this data (see Figure 3-3). This is an important step, as in some companies not every person who has access to Google Analytics data should have access to AdSense data. Either some employees should not have access to revenue data (but still have access to behavior data) or the company works with service providers who should not have access to this data.

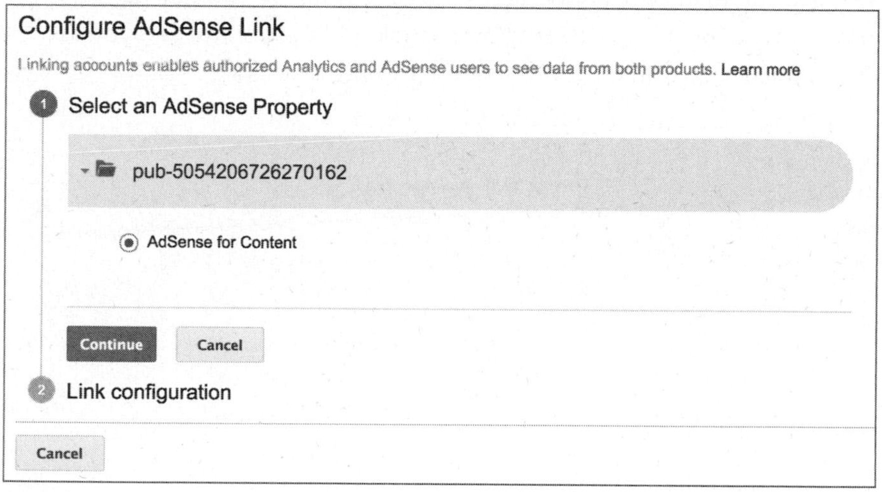

**Figure 3-2:** Choosing an AdSense property to link to Google Analytics

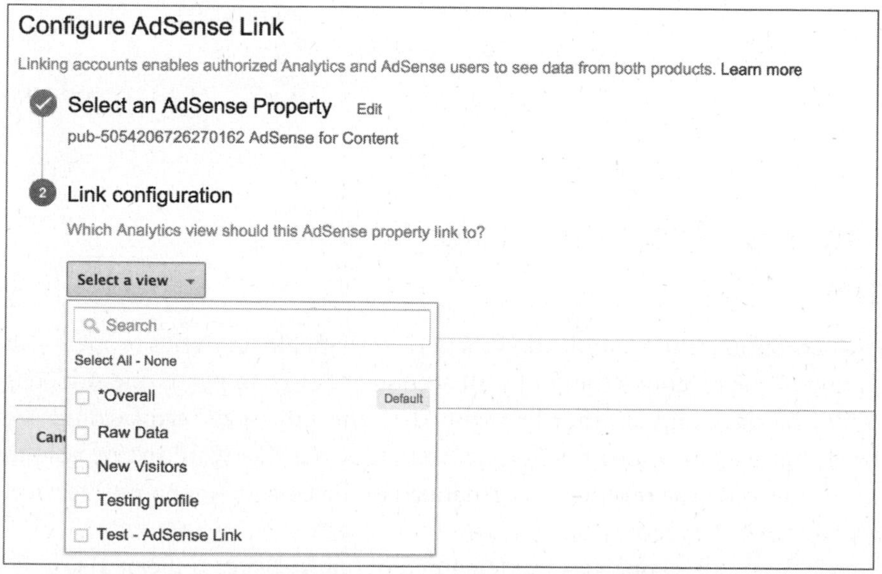

**Figure 3-3:** Choosing which Google Analytics views will report AdSense data

In cases where access to AdSense is not open to every Google Analytics user, I recommend that you create a separate Google Analytics view (see the guide at `http://goo.gl/MSVGW6`) where you have all the necessary settings discussed in Chapter 1, "Implementation Best Practices," excluding the AdSense data. This will help you manage who has access to your AdSense revenue data.

Once you choose which views will report on AdSense data, click on Enable Link and you are done! Figure 3-4 shows the summary page when you finish the linking process.

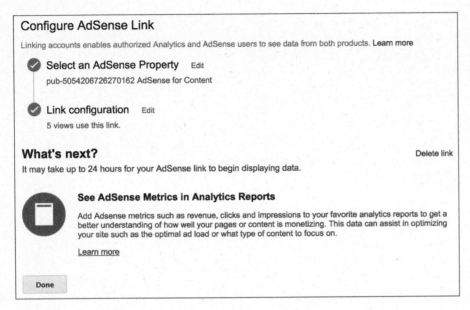

**Figure 3-4:** AdSense linking summary

## Linking Multiple AdSense Accounts and/or Google Analytics Properties

If you have multiple AdSense accounts, you can link all of them to one Google Analytics property; in this case, you would see a sum of the revenue brought by all accounts. For example, if one AdSense account brought $2 in a specific page and another brought $1 to the same page, you would see $3 revenue originating from that page reported on Google Analytics, but you wouldn't be able to determine from which AdSense account the revenue was generated in the Google Analytics interface. For that you need to check your AdSense reports at `www.google.com/adsense`.

If you have multiple Google Analytics properties implemented in one website, you can also link all of them to one AdSense account. In this case you would see the data attributed across all Google Analytics properties as reported on AdSense. For example, if you have two Google Analytics properties implemented in a specific page that generated $2 of revenue in a specific time range, you would see $2 attributed to it in both Google Analytics property reports.

It is also important to note that once you link the accounts, you will still be able to access each product separately and provide access to data only to the people that need it. For example, if you want people to have access to Google Analytics only, you can still do that (check Step 4) or you can provide access only to AdSense through its interface as well.

## Unlinking and Managing Access to Data

In order to manage or unlink AdSense from Google Analytics, follow the steps described in Step 2 to reach the Product Linking section. You will reach a page similar to Figure 3-5.

| + NEW ADSENSE LINK | Q Search |
| --- | --- |
| **AdSense Account**          ↓ | **AdSense Web Property** |
| pub-5054206726270162 | AdSense for Content |
| | |

**Figure 3-5:** Linked AdSense accounts to a Google Analytics property

When you click on the AdSense Publisher ID, you will reach a page similar to Figure 3-4. From there, you can edit your link configuration both by choosing a different Publisher ID linked to your user or by changing which views have access to your AdSense data.

In addition, if you want to delete the link between the accounts, you will see a link on this page to Delete Link. Click the link and you will receive a popup to confirm if you would like to unlink the accounts. Note that if you decide to delete the link, Google Analytics will stop receiving data from AdSense, but data up until the time you unlink the property will still be available. It is not possible to delete data that was already collected.

## Data Discrepancies Between Google Analytics and AdSense

If you performed the process just described, you should have your reports populated with accurate AdSense data. However, sometimes stats might differ between the two platforms. This list describes the top five reasons for discrepancies in the data. Please take a few minutes to go over it to minimize the chances that your data will be inaccurate.

- **Missing code:** The Google Analytics tracking code or the AdSense tag may not be implemented in all website pages. This can result in large differences between the two tools. In order to check whether there is a difference in the number of pages with AdSense and Google Analytics implemented, you can use the Web Analytics Solution Provider crawler available at the Chrome Store at http://goo.gl/UbcJXa.
- **View filters:** As suggested in Chapter 1, a common technique used on Google Analytics to segment users is to create different reporting views. These views are filtered to exclude specific data to customize your reports. AdSense data associated with sessions that are filtered out of a

Google Analytics view are also excluded from all Google Analytics reports in that view. Learn more about view filters at `http://goo.gl/Egc6QE`.

- **Browser support and configuration**: AdSense uses an iframe to serve ads, so there might be issues with browsers that do not support iframes. This can be a common issue in mobile browsers. In addition, users might have technology installed in their browsers that blocks AdSense ads (such as extensions and firewalls). In both cases, you would see more pageviews on Google Analytics than page impressions on AdSense.
- **Time zones and sync**: The AdSense team updates its reports more often than it sends data to Google Analytics reports, so AdSense data will always be fresher when it comes to its own metrics. Also, it will take 24 hours from the moment you link the accounts for data to start being populated in Google Analytics. Last, if your time zones are set differently for each product, the data will be aggregated differently, resulting in discrepancies in the data.
- **Non-supported AdSense products**: As mentioned, the integration is valid only for AdSense for content, so if you are also using AdSense to monetize search boxes, mobile units, or any other product, be sure to compare only the content ad units.

## Analyzing AdSense Effectiveness Using Google Analytics

In this section, you learn about the default reports you get as a result of the integration; you also learn advanced techniques to use standard Google Analytics features to analyze your AdSense performance. But before diving into the reports, let's look at the metrics that will be available on Google Analytics after the integration:

- **AdSense Revenue***: Revenue generated by AdSense ads.
- **Ads Clicked***: The number of times AdSense ads were clicked.
- **AdSense CTR (click-through rate)**: The percentage of page impressions that resulted in a click on an ad.
- **AdSense eCPM**: The estimated cost per thousand page impressions; it is your AdSense Revenue per 1,000 page impressions.
- **AdSense Page Impressions***: The number of pageviews during which an ad was displayed (a page impression can have multiple ad units).
- **AdSense Ad Units Viewed***: Number of ad units viewed (an ad unit is a set of ads displayed as a result of one piece of the AdSense ad code).
- **AdSense Impressions***: Number of ads viewed (multiple ads can be displayed in an ad unit).
- **AdSense Exits***: The number of sessions that ended due to a user clicking on an AdSense ad.
- **AdSense Viewable Impressions Percent**: The percentage of viewable impressions.
- **AdSense Coverage**: The percentage of ad requests that returned at least one ad.

*These metrics can be segmented using the Segment Builder on the Google Analytics interface.*

In the following sections, you learn about the reports and analyses that can be performed using the integration between Google Analytics and AdSense, starting from the default AdSense reports and proceeding to more advanced ways to analyze data using Google Analytics features.

## AdSense Overview

This report provides a bird's-eye view, including all AdSense metrics available in Google Analytics. You can reach the report by visiting http://goo.gl/dEZa22 or on Google Analytics's left sidebar under the Behavior section. By default, the line chart displays the total daily AdSense revenue for your site, but you can graph any two metrics by choosing them on the top-left drop-down above the graph.

In addition, the overview report can be segmented using the Segment Builder, which is an effective way to compare two to four different groups of users (learn more about it at http://goo .gl/Us97e8). In Figure 3-6, you can see such a comparison, where each line represents a different age group—18–34, 35–54, and 55+. As you can see, it is possible to understand the trends for each segment at a glimpse.

**Figure 3-6:** AdSense overview report with segments

If you want to perform the same analysis, you can import those three segments into your Google Analytics account by following these links:

- Age 18–34: `http://goo.gl/jY8DOF`
- Age 35–54: `http://goo.gl/2s3UjE`
- Age 55+: `http://goo.gl/Xtt3K8`

**NOTE** In order to receive demographic data in your account, you might need to change your settings. Here is an article explaining how: `http://goo.gl/eh7WnM`.

## AdSense Pages

This report provides information about the pages that contributed most to AdSense revenue. It will show each of the pages on the website and how well they performed in terms of AdSense.

As you can see in Figure 3-7, for each page in the website that contains an AdSense unit, you can analyze the following metrics: AdSense revenue, AdSense ads clicked, AdSense CTR, AdSense eCPM, AdSense impressions, and AdSense page impressions. If you want to have all AdSense metrics in one single table, you can import such a custom report by following this link: `http://goo.gl/rHneN6`. This might be useful if you are interested in downloading or emailing your AdSense report.

| Page | AdSense Revenue ↓ | AdSense Ads Clicked | AdSense CTR | AdSense eCPM | AdSense Impressions | AdSense Page Impressions |
|---|---|---|---|---|---|---|
| | **$2,311.87** % of Total: 100.00% ($2,311.87) | **2,634** % of Total: 100.00% (2,634) | **0.37%** Site Avg: 0.37% (0.00%) | **$3.23** Site Avg: $3.23 (0.00%) | **1,799,851** % of Total: 100.00% (1,799,851) | **716,790** % of Total: 100.00% (716,790) |
| 1. /analytics/google-tag-manager | $204.29 (8.84%) | 197 (7.48%) | 0.32% | $3.32 | 179,155 (9.95%) | 61,559 (8.59%) |
| 2. /analytics/in-page | $137.03 (5.93%) | 117 (4.44%) | 0.53% | $6.24 | 56,843 (3.16%) | 21,962 (3.06%) |
| 3. / | $113.10 (4.89%) | 147 (5.58%) | 0.39% | $3.00 | 47,298 (2.63%) | 37,735 (5.26%) |
| 4. /analytics/demographics | $101.14 (4.37%) | 103 (3.91%) | 0.32% | $3.14 | 95,175 (5.29%) | 32,240 (4.50%) |
| 5. /testing/content-experiments | $71.47 (3.09%) | 97 (3.68%) | 0.35% | $2.58 | 79,851 (4.44%) | 27,712 (3.87%) |

**Figure 3-7:** AdSense pages report

Note that in the top-left corner of the table in Figure 3-7, you will find a drop-down where you can choose a secondary dimension. This will allow you to add an extra dimension that can be used to segment the primary dimension shown in the table.

So, for example, if you are interested in seeing, for each page, if there is a difference in performance based on gender, you would choose Gender as the secondary dimension. Figure 3-8 shows how the resulting table would look for such an analysis. This example uncovers that while female sessions result in less revenue for this specific article, this happens because the female audience is smaller. Females actually have both a higher CTR and a higher eCPM.

| Primary Dimension: Page | | | | | | | | |
|---|---|---|---|---|---|---|---|---|
| Secondary dimension: Gender ▼   Sort Type: Default ▼ | | | | google-tag-manager | advanced | | | |
| Page | Gender | AdSense Revenue | AdSense Ads Clicked | AdSense CTR | AdSense eCPM | AdSense Impressions | AdSense Page Impressions |
| | | $151.64 % of Total: 6.56% ($2,311.87) | 105 % of Total: 3.99% (2,634) | 0.37% Site Avg: 0.37% (0.24%) | $5.32 Site Avg: $3.23 (84.94%) | 83,492 % of Total: 4.64% (1,799,851) | 28,504 % of Total: 3.98% (716,790) |
| 1.  /analytics/google-tag-manager | male | $114.47 (75.49%) | 80 (76.19%) | 0.36% | $5.10 | 66,160 (79.24%) | 22,464 (78.81%) |
| 2.  /analytics/google-tag-manager | female | $37.16 (24.51%) | 25 (23.81%) | 0.41% | $6.15 | 17,332 (20.76%) | 6,040 (21.19%) |

**Figure 3-8:** AdSense Pages report segmented by gender

This report provides an interesting view of which page performed best, and it can be used to optimize website content. For example, if you find that posts about celebrities generate more revenue than posts about football, you might consider writing more about celebrities (if your main objective is making money through AdSense).

However, using *Content Grouping* is a more scalable approach to optimize AdSense placements and content categories to generate more revenue. Content Grouping is a Google Analytics feature that lets you group content into a logical structure that reflects your business needs. Once you define Content Groupings, you will be able to compare aggregated metrics by group name. Most websites work with templates and each template may have different AdSense placements. This means that an important analysis would be to compare performance by template (or by category) rather than by page.

In order to analyze template performance, you need to create a Content Grouping for it. There are three ways to do so:

- Modify the tracking code on each page you want to group
- Extract pages with regex capture groups
- Create rules to include pages in a group

This example uses the third option, but you can learn more about the other options at http://goo.gl/yXMscZ. Suppose your website has the following page templates:

- Article pages with URLs including /analytics/ or /testing/
- Video pages with URLs including /videos/
- Cartoon pages with URLs including /cartoons/
- Homepage with the URL /

In this case, click on Admin on the top of the Google Analytics reporting interface and search for Content Grouping below the view you want to create the group for. Click on it and then click on + New Content Grouping, and name it in a way that will make sense when analyzing your data. Figure 3-9 shows the configuration for this example.

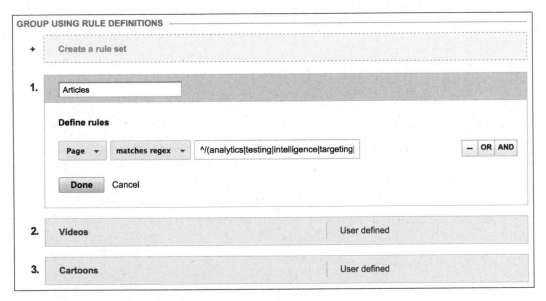

**Figure 3-9:** Creating Content Grouping for AdSense analysis

After creating the Content Grouping based on your website structure (such as content type, content category, content authors, and so on), you will be able to choose them in many reports. However, it might be a better approach to create a custom report, where you can choose the metrics and dimensions you want to analyze alongside your AdSense performance. An example of how to configure such a custom report is shown in Figure 3-10. To reach the configuration page, visit http://goo.gl/q4dxOn and click on + New Custom Report (note that you can return to the previous URL in the future to find all your custom reports).

The configuration shown in Figure 3-10 will create a custom report where the primary dimension is the Content Grouping defined in Figure 3-9 (named Content Type). In addition, by clicking on a group you can drill down to the specific pages inside that group and see how they performed for the same metrics.

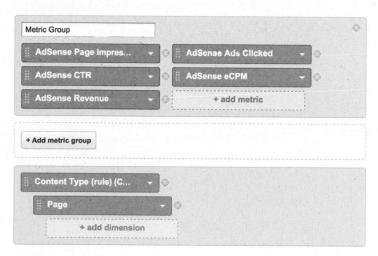

**Figure 3-10:** Custom report with Content Grouping and AdSense

Figure 3-11 shows the final table, where you see the main AdSense metrics per Content Type (the Content Group defined in Figure 3-9). This table serves as a bird's eye view to how content performs on the website when it comes to AdSense (you might also want to add metrics to broaden the scope of the table).

In Figure 3-11 you can see, for example, that while the Analytics section has higher revenue, this is a consequence of a significantly higher number of impressions. When you analyze the table further, you see that the Videos section has the greatest potential, with a higher CTR (more than 50%) and AdSense eCPM. Based on these metrics, you can understand which templates or types of content are the most effective.

| Content Type (rule) (Content Group) ? | AdSense Page Impressions ? ↓ | AdSense Ads Clicked ? | AdSense CTR ? | AdSense eCPM ? | AdSense Revenue ? |
|---|---|---|---|---|---|
| | **427,051**<br>% of Total: 94.07%<br>(453,986) | **1,547**<br>% of Total:<br>98.41% (1,572) | **0.36%**<br>Site Avg:<br>0.35%<br>(4.62%) | **$3.34**<br>Site Avg:<br>$3.24<br>(2.86%) | **$1,424.27**<br>% of Total: 96.76%<br>($1,472.02) |
| 1. Articles | **338,018** (79.15%) | 1,344 (86.88%) | 0.40% | $3.83 | $1,293.21 (90.80%) |
| 2. eBooks | **32,584** (7.63%) | 36 (2.33%) | 0.11% | $0.27 | $8.73 (0.61%) |
| 3. Cartoons | **20,352** (4.77%) | 13 (0.84%) | 0.06% | $0.09 | $1.88 (0.13%) |
| 4. Home | **16,793** (3.93%) | 79 (5.11%) | 0.47% | $3.59 | $60.26 (4.23%) |
| 5. Videos | **9,363** (2.19%) | 62 (4.01%) | 0.66% | $5.20 | $48.69 (3.42%) |

**Figure 3-11:** Analyzing AdSense performance with Content Grouping

# AdSense Referrers

This report provides information about the performance of referral traffic that brought users to the website when it comes to AdSense revenue (direct link: http://goo.gl/xkMPbo). This information is extremely valuable; however, I suggest using a different report, which is part of the standard reports and provides more in-depth information about acquisition performance. Visit the All Traffic report at http://goo.gl/otYhAr and click on AdSense in the Metric group selector, as shown in Figure 3-12.

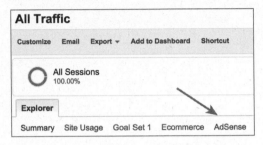

**Figure 3-12:** All Traffic report with AdSense metrics

From this report, you can analyze the sources, mediums, campaigns, or any other dimension on Google Analytics (such as browser, country, landing pages, and so on) that are driving revenue on AdSense; this can be done through the Primary Dimension selector. Here is an example of one interesting way to analyze this data.

A. **Choose a primary dimension:** This is the dimension used to analyze the metrics, the first column of the table. You can choose almost any dimension existent on Google Analytics, but some are especially interesting, such as:

- *Source/Medium:* Shows which traffic sources are the most profitable.
- *Keyword:* Shows paid keywords generating revenue; can be an important metric when building a PPC strategy.
- *Landing Page:* Shows through which landing page visitors that clicked on AdSense entered the website.
- *Country:* Provides insight into optimization based on country; for example, countries with languages from right-to-left (like Hebrew) might show a significantly different click behavior on AdSense.
- *Visitor Type:* Shows whether visitors who clicked on an ad are new or returning visitors. This can show if AdSense should be more prominent to new or returning visitors.

**B.** **Choose a secondary dimension:** The secondary dimension allows you to view the primary dimension drilled down by another dimension within the same table. It basically adds another level of detail to the report.

**C.** **Choose a visualization type:** The visualization will be essential in order to understand the data; it can be a table, a pie chart, a bar chart, a comparison chart, a cloud, or a pivot table.

Figure 3-13 shows an interesting visualization to analyze AdSense performance by GEO location (the letters A, B, and C show the steps explained previously). You can see, for example, that in the United States returning visitors are more likely to click through than new visitors in the same country. You can also see that while the United States has a higher overall revenue, Australia's new visitors might be a good opportunity, with a CTR 83% higher than the website average.

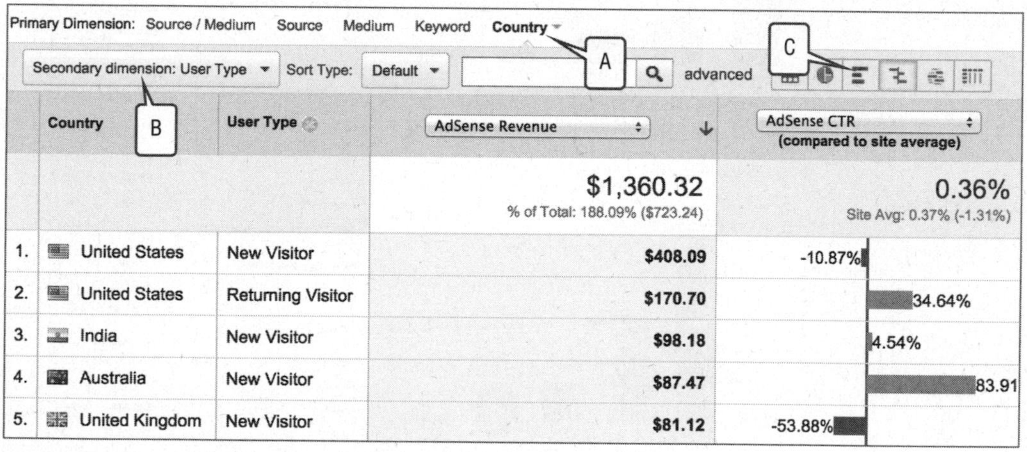

| | Country | User Type | AdSense Revenue | AdSense CTR (compared to site average) |
|---|---|---|---|---|
| | | | **$1,360.32** % of Total: 188.09% ($723.24) | **0.36%** Site Avg: 0.37% (-1.31%) |
| 1. | United States | New Visitor | **$408.09** | -10.87% |
| 2. | United States | Returning Visitor | **$170.70** | 34.64% |
| 3. | India | New Visitor | **$98.18** | 4.54% |
| 4. | Australia | New Visitor | **$87.47** | 83.91 |
| 5. | United Kingdom | New Visitor | **$81.12** | -53.88% |

**Figure 3-13:** GEO location performance by AdSense metrics

# Google Analytics Dashboard to Monitor AdSense Performance

Dashboards are a comfortable and sometimes effective way to monitor the performance of a website. A good dashboard aggregates all the necessary information in one place for quick access. And since Google Analytics offers the capability to create and share dashboards, I created the one in Figure 3-14 to help you monitor your AdSense performance.

The dashboard in Figure 3-14 can be used to measure your most profitable channels, pages, and demographics when it comes to AdSense revenue. You can add the dashboard to your Google

Analytics account by following `http://goo.gl/c031f8` (make sure you are signed in to your Google Analytics account before clicking).

Each column of the dashboard in Figure 3-14 has a theme. The first column shows overall performance metrics over time (widgets 1–4); the second focuses on demographics (widgets 5–7); and the third shows important information on behavior and acquisition (widgets 8–10). You will learn more about each widget in the next sections.

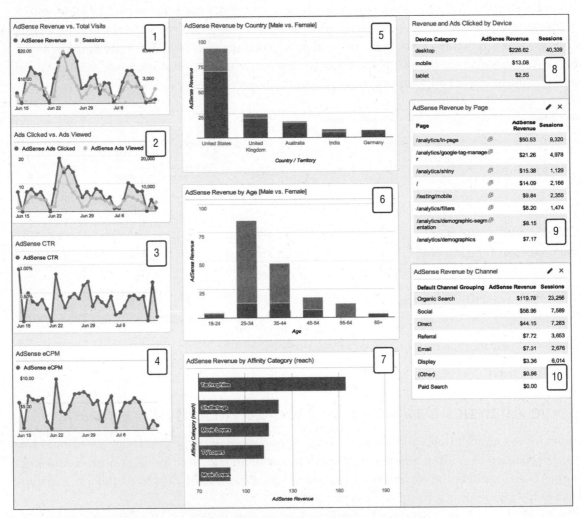

**Figure 3-14:** Google Analytics dashboard for monitoring AdSense performance

## Overall Performance Trends (Widgets 1–4)

Widgets 1–4 are visualized in the first column of Figure 3-14 using line charts; this data visualization type is most effective when visualizing trends and small changes in data, which makes sense when looking at performance trends over time. Following is an explanation of each of the widgets:

- **Widget 1: AdSense Revenue vs. Total Sessions:** Shows the overall performance of the website. If you see diverging trends on the lines, it means that something worth checking is happening. Drill down into it.
- **Widget 2. Ads Clicked vs. Ads Viewed:** Shows a trend of the absolute number of ads people are viewing on the website and how many of them are being clicked.
- **Widget 3. AdSense CTR:** Summarizes widget 2. The click-through rate (CTR) is the percentage of page impressions that resulted in a click on an ad. You definitely want to see an upward trend.
- **Widget 4. AdSense eCPM:** The AdSense eCPM is the estimated cost per thousand page impressions. It is your AdSense revenue per 1,000 page impressions, which is a great performance metric.

## Demographic Segments (Widgets 5–7)

Widgets 5–7 are visualized in the second column of Figure 3-14 using bar charts; this data visualization type is most effective when showing comparisons among categories, which makes it a good option to visualize the differences between segments of users. Following is an explanation of each of the widgets:

- **Widget 5. AdSense Revenue by Country [Male vs. Female]:** This stacked bar chart shows the AdSense revenue per country, and each bar is divided between Males (blue) and Females (green). As you can see in this example, Australia and Germany are heavily biased toward men, so a good tactic might be to find content that is particularly appealing to women and promote it on the homepage of those countries.
- **Widget 6. AdSense Revenue by Age [Male vs. Female]:** This stacked bar chart shows AdSense revenue per age group, and each bar is divided between Males (blue) and Females (green). In the example, you can see that very old and very young visitors are heavily biased toward men, but all other age groups are biased toward females, especially 55–64. Again, it might be interesting to run a content analysis and adjust content strategy based on that.
- **Widget 7. AdSense Revenue by Affinity Category:** This bar chart shows the AdSense revenue per affinity category. This information might help you understand which groups are the most interesting in terms of revenue, and might help drive the content strategy for the website.

> **NOTE**  Widgets 5–7 depend on having demographics enabled for your account. Learn more about it at http://goo.gl/eXGbmX.

### Behavior and Acquisition (Widgets 8–10)

Widgets 8–10 are visualized in the third column of Figure 3-14 using tables, the most effective way to present detailed data on dimensions and metrics; tables make a good option to visualize acquisition channels and content consumption. Following is an explanation of each of the widgets:

- **Widget 8. Revenue and Ads Clicked by Device:** We live on a mobile planet, so it is important to check if your ads are being clicked and are generating revenue on all devices at a similar rate.
- **Widget 9. AdSense Revenue by Page:** This table is a great indicator of which content is performing well and how much time you should invest in each topic.
- **Widget 10. AdSense Revenue by Channel:** This table shows which acquisition channel is bringing the most profitable visitors.

> **NOTE**  To download the dashboard, visit http://goo.gl/c031f8.

## Summary

In this chapter you learned about the integration between Google Analytics and AdSense. This integration is very helpful as it enables publishers to use advanced Google Analytics features in order to understand and optimize AdSense performance for a website.

A few recommendations:

- Understand which content type and subject generates the highest revenue and create content based on this data.
- Understand which page templates bring the best results by segmenting your data with both Content Grouping and the Segments feature.
- Analyze AdSense performance to learn which segments have a good CTR; this might bring insight into which audience to target.

# 4

# Mobile Apps Integrations

Google Analytics provides a mobile app measurement platform that empowers app owners, marketers, and developers to analyze user interaction on both Android and iOS, allowing a better understanding of user engagement with apps. The platform can provide insightful information, such as device types and brands, time spent on screens, crashes and exceptions, in-app purchases, and others.

However, unlike with the web, user acquisition does not happen through the app itself. It happens through one of the available app markets, mainly Google Play and iTunes. This means that app developers have less control over marketing measurement. That's why Google Analytics developed integrations for both markets, so that app owners, marketers, and developers can better measure campaign performance and link this information to post-installation interactions. The information acquired through these integrations will enable you to optimize campaigns not only for installs, but also for actual purchases and other meaningful metrics.

In this chapter, you learn how to set up the Google Analytics' install tracking feature for both Android and iOS, which will populate the acquisition sources and the Google Play Referral Flow reports in Google Analytics. You also learn techniques that will help you better understand the reports and extract insights from them.

## Viewing Google Play and iTunes Data on Google Analytics

The steps for setting up install tracking are different for Android and iOS, but they are both relatively straightforward, requiring few code changes. The following sections include a step-by-step guide for each of them. Note that this guide refers to version 4 of the Android SDK and version 3 of the iOS SDK. If you don't know which version you are using, ask your developer. You can download the Android SDK from `http://goo.gl/mpF073` and the iOS SDK from `http://goo.gl/wmZfni`.

But before you begin, it is important you make sure you are measuring your customers' interactions properly, so that you not only have the SDK running, but you also have your business questions answered. This will allow you to link the data you get from Google Play and iTunes in a more meaningful way. Following is a list of important questions you might want to answer; you can find the necessary code to implement them at `http://goo.gl/H1t2yC`.

- What actions are my users performing?
- How much money are users spending in my app?
- Are users completing my app objectives?
- How do users with a specific trait behave?
- How long does it take for a user to accomplish a task?

In order to make use of the Mobile App measurement platform and the integrations discussed in this chapter, you will need to set up an App View. When you set up a Property, you will be prompted to set up an App View; select this option. This allows you to see your app data in reports that best reflect the app experience. If you want to take advantage of the integrations discussed here (and other app-only features), you will need to choose the app option.

If you want your data captured both in an app-specific view as well as a view that captures both app and web, send your data to two different properties—the one that houses just app data and the one that houses all data. Alternatively, you can make use of the rollup property (a feature available in Google Analytics Premium) to roll all your data up to one place. You can read more about it at `http://goo.gl/V74xx1`.

It is important to note that if you combine website and app analytics data, you should use the User ID feature (discussed in-depth in Part II of the book). This will allow you to see cross-device performance in relation to your website and app in a single view. If you choose this solution, you will be able to filter out web and app hits into separate views for better analyses, as shown at `http://goo.gl/9e8Sk0`.

> **NOTE**    I warmly recommend that you check out the Mobile App Analytics Fundamentals course at the Analytics Academy. It will provide you with a strong foundation and help you succeed with mobile app measurement. You can find the course at `http://goo.gl/Ts9SKB`.

# Android SDK v4: Setting Up Install Tracking and Campaign Measurement

The process of setting up Install Tracking and Campaign Measurement is straightforward, and even though they can be implemented independently, it is highly recommended that you implement both of them, as they have a highly synergetic nature. Install Tracking enables you to view app data from Google Play in your Google Analytics Property, while Campaign Measurement makes your Acquisition more accurate and complete. Both are extremely important.

The following four steps are discussed in this section:

1. Link your Apps to your Google Analytics property.
2. Update your `AndroidManifest.xml` file.
3. Add campaign parameters to your Google Play links.
4. Customize the Android SDK to General Campaign Tracking and Traffic Source Attribution.

## Step 1: Link Your Apps to Your Google Analytics Property

The first step necessary to get Google Play data into Google Analytics is to link your apps to your Google Analytics property in the Admin section of your account. To do that, log in to your account and click on Admin at the top of your screen. Then choose the property that you want to link to your app (since the linking is at the property level, all views in the property will show this data) and click on Property Settings. You will see a control similar to Figure 4-1.

> **Get Google Play Developer Console Data**
>
> **Link Apps From Google Play**
> Use Google Analytics to see how many times people view or download your app from Google Play.
>
> [ OFF ]

**Figure 4-1:** Linking control for Android SDK

Once you turn it on, you can choose which of your apps you would like to link to Google Analytics. Only someone with Edit permission in Google Analytics who uses the same email address in the Play Developer Console can proceed to link the accounts. If that's the case, you will be given a list of apps, similar to the one in Figure 4-2. Choose the app(s) you want to link to your Google Analytics property.

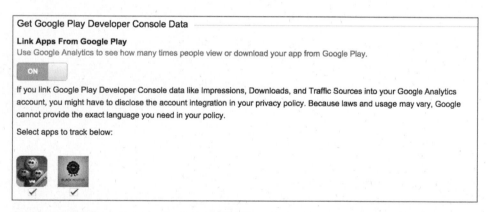

**Figure 4-2:** App selection from Google Play

> **NOTE**   Figure 4-2 was kindly provided by JiaJing Wang, Software Engineer at Google. You might want to try this game—it is quite fun! Visit `http://goo.gl/dO3OVM`.

## Step 2: Update Your AndroidManifest.xml File

Once the Google Analytics settings are out of your way, you need to update a few lines of code in your `AndroidManifest.xml` file. This code will add a `BroadcastReceiver` to your app so that it can receive and set the campaign information contained in the referral link (discussed later in this chapter). The code follows, but you can copy/paste it from the following link `http://goo.gl/9T9lrK`:

```
<!-- Used for Google Play Store Campaign Measurement-->;
<service
    android:name="com.google.android.gms.analytics.CampaignTrackingService" />
<receiver
    android:name="com.google.android.gms.analytics.CampaignTrackingReceiver"
    android:exported="true">
<intent-filter>
    <action android:name="com.android.vending.INSTALL_REFERRER" />
</intent-filter>
</receiver>
```

## Step 3: Add Campaign Parameters to Your Google Play Links

You learned about campaign tagging best practices using UTM parameters in Chapter 1, "Implementation Best Practices," and the same principles apply for Android apps. You should *always* have campaign parameters when sending potential customers to Google Play; well, except when you are sending them through Google AdWords, in which case you should only enable Auto Tagging. But in addition to the URL parameters discussed in Chapter 1, you will need to add the package name.

I usually recommend using the Google Play URL Builder (Figure 4-3) to build links for campaigns; you can find it at `http://goo.gl/I3rTnI`.

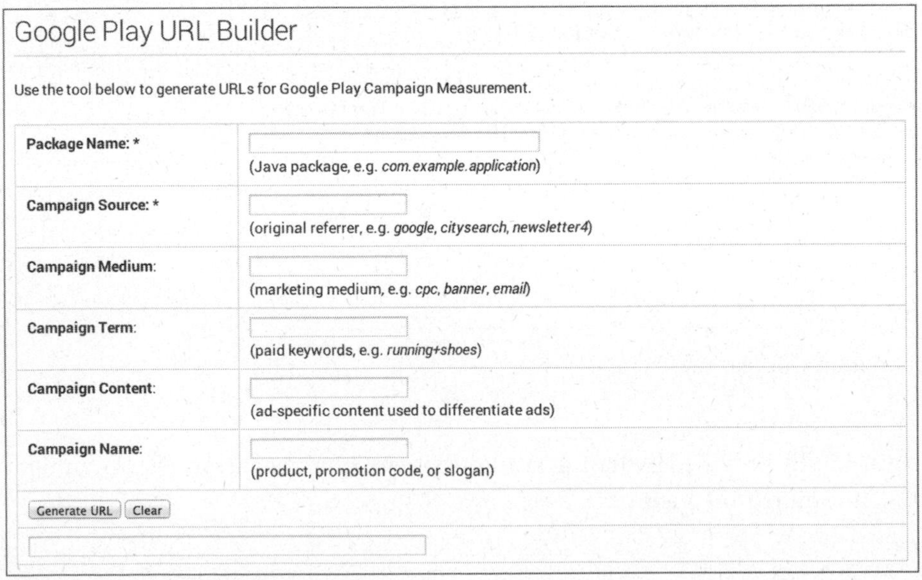

**Figure 4-3:** Google Play URL Builder

However, for companies advertising through dozens or hundreds of different campaigns and networks, it might become unrealistic to build one URL at a time. In such cases, I recommend using a spreadsheet template where you have all the parameters' values and a concatenate function that creates the final link. Figure 4-4 shows a sample spreadsheet. You can download a template from `http://goo.gl/CO5tdu`, a solution developed by Cardinal Path, a Google Analytics Certified Partner and Google Analytics Premium reseller. (You need to be signed in to a Google account in order for this link to work.)

| | A | B | C | D | E | F | G | H |
|---|---|---|---|---|---|---|---|---|
| 1 | *required | | | *required | | | | Click minify from the Menu |
| 2 | DESTINATION URL | CAMPAIGN NAME | TRAFFIC SOURCE | MEDIUM | KEYWORD | AD CONTENT | TAGGED URL | MINIFIED URL |
| 3 | http://www.cardinalpath.com | GA Premium Webinar | spreadsheet | banner | | | http://www.cardinalpath.com/?utm_campaign=GA%20| | http://goo.gl/6H14qr |
| 4 | http://www.cardinalpath.com/blog | GA Premium Webinar | spreadsheet | QR banner | | | http://www.cardinalpath.com/blog?utm_campaign=GA5 | http://goo.gl/U6RC4r |
| 5 | | | | | | | | |
| 6 | | | | | | | | |

**Figure 4-4:** Google Play URL Builder spreadsheet

## Step 4: Customize the Android SDK to General Campaign Tracking and Traffic Source Attribution

The previous steps discussed ways to attribute the source of users coming to Google Play right before installing your app (such as for new users). While this information is critical in order to measure campaign success, you also want to capture the traffic sources for subsequent user sessions. This will enable you to understand how well your retention marketing is working.

In order to capture traffic sources for users who land directly in your app, you need to tag your links as described in Step 3, so that Google Analytics understands where the user is coming from. In addition to that, you need to set the campaign parameters on your tracker through the `setCampaignParamsFromUrl` method, as exemplified here (source `http://goo.gl/bCvzpg`):

```
// Get tracker.
Tracker
  t = ((AnalyticsSampleApp) getActivity().getApplication()).getTracker(
  TrackerName.APP_TRACKER);
// Set screen name.
t.setScreenName(screenName);

// In this example, campaign information is set using
// an url string with Google Analytics campaign parameters.
// Note: This is for illustrative purposes. In most cases campaign
// information would come from an incoming Intent.
String campaignData = "http://examplepetstore.com/index.html?" +
"utm_source=email&utm_medium=email_marketing&utm_campaign=summer" +
"&utm_content=email_variation_1";

// Campaign data sent with this hit.
t.send(new HitBuilders.ScreenViewBuilder()
      .setCampaignParamsFromUrl(campaignData)
      .build()
      );
```

# iOS SDK v3: Setting Up Install Tracking and Campaign Measurement

One important note regarding iOS data is that a user must download, install, and launch an app in order for the referring source data to appear in the reports. This means that if 1,000 users come from a campaign to your iTunes description page, 600 end up installing it, and 500 hundred end up launching it, you will see the 500 hundred attributed to the campaign. You won't see data for the remaining 500 hundred.

The same note mentioned in the previous section about Android Install Tracking and Campaign Measurement importance also applies to iOS; they are both extremely important. Below are the four steps discussed in this section:

1. Enable iOS Campaign Tracking in Your Google Analytics property.
2. Add the `libAdIdAccess.a` library to your XCode project.
3. Add campaign parameters to your links to iTunes.
4. Customize the iOS SDK to General Campaign Tracking and Traffic Source Attribution.

## Step 1: Enable iOS Campaign Tracking in Your Google Analytics Property

The first step necessary to get iTunes data into Google Analytics is to enable the campaign-tracking features for your Google Analytics property in the Admin section of your account. To do that, log in to your account and click on Admin at the top of your screen. Then choose the property that you want to link to your app (since the linking is at the property level, all views in the property will show this data) and click on Property Settings. You will see a snippet similar to Figure 4-5. Turn campaign tracking on and proceed to Step 2.

**Figure 4-5:** Linking control for iOS campaign tracking

## Step 2: Add the libAdIdAccess.a Library to Your XCode Project

There is only one code change required for app developers to set up install tracking for iOS, which will allow access to the iOS identifier for advertising (IDFA). To enable IDFA collection, link the related files and set the `allowIDFACollection` property to `YES` on each tracker that will collect the IDFA. Here is the line of code to be added:

```
// Enable IDFA collection.
tracker.allowIDFACollection = YES;
```

Refer to the `README` file in the SDK for more information.

## Step 3: Add Campaign Parameters to Your Links to iTunes

This step is very similar to Google Play's instructions for Android as described in Step 3 in the previous section. The only difference is that iOS links will require additional parameters: Google Analytics Property ID, Ad Network, and Redirect URL. You can find the iOS Campaign Tracking URL Builder (see Figure 4-6) at `http://goo.gl/Arg8tw`.

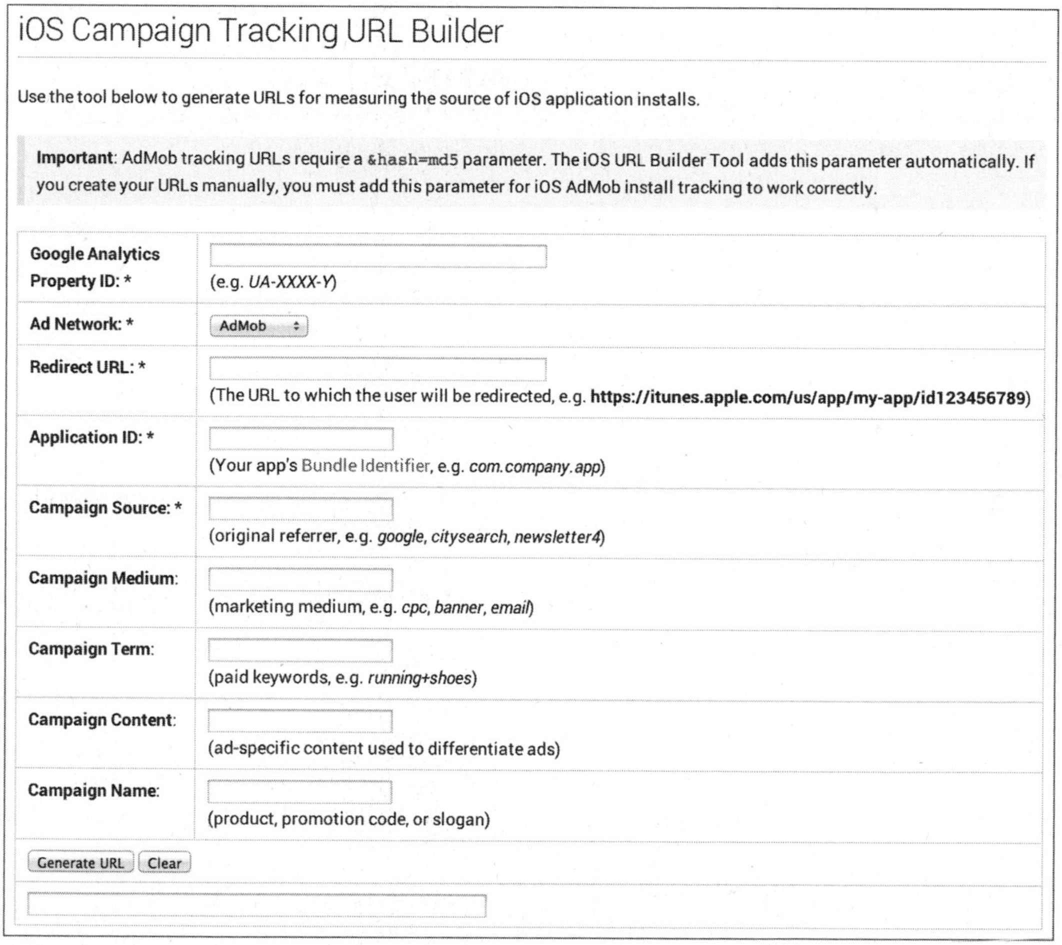

iOS Campaign Tracking URL Builder

Use the tool below to generate URLs for measuring the source of iOS application installs.

**Important**: AdMob tracking URLs require a `&hash=md5` parameter. The iOS URL Builder Tool adds this parameter automatically. If you create your URLs manually, you must add this parameter for iOS AdMob install tracking to work correctly.

| | |
|---|---|
| **Google Analytics Property ID: *** | (e.g. *UA-XXXX-Y*) |
| **Ad Network: *** | AdMob ⇕ |
| **Redirect URL: *** | (The URL to which the user will be redirected, e.g. **https://itunes.apple.com/us/app/my-app/id123456789**) |
| **Application ID: *** | (Your app's Bundle Identifier, e.g. *com.company.app*) |
| **Campaign Source: *** | (original referrer, e.g. *google, citysearch, newsletter4*) |
| **Campaign Medium**: | (marketing medium, e.g. *cpc, banner, email*) |
| **Campaign Term**: | (paid keywords, e.g. *running+shoes*) |
| **Campaign Content**: | (ad-specific content used to differentiate ads) |
| **Campaign Name**: | (product, promotion code, or slogan) |

Generate URL    Clear

**Figure 4-6:** iOS Campaign Tracking URL Builder

## Step 4: Customize the iOS SDK to General Campaign Tracking and Traffic Source Attribution

Similarly to the process described for Google Play (Step 4 from the previous section), in order to capture traffic sources for users who land directly in your app (after installing it, in subsequent sessions), you will still need to tag your links as described in Step 3 so that Google Analytics understands where the user comes from. In addition to that, you also need to use `[GAIDictionaryBuilder setCampaignParametersFromUrl:urlString]`, where `urlString` is a string representing an URL that may contain Google Analytics campaign parameters. Here is an example of how to do it (for the source, go to `http://goo.gl/KHVs17`):

```
/*
* MyAppDelegate.m
*
* An example of how to implement campaign and referral attribution. If no
* Google Analytics campaign parameters are set in the referring URL, use the
* hostname as a referrer instead.
*/

- (BOOL)application:(UIApplication *)application handleOpenURL:(NSURL *) url {

NSString *urlString = [url absoluteString];

id<GAITracker> tracker = [[GAI sharedInstance]
   trackerWithName:@"tracker" trackingId:@"UA-XXXX-Y"];

// setCampaignParametersFromUrl: parses Google Analytics campaign
// ("UTM")parameters from a string url into a Map that can be set on a Tracker.

GAIDictionaryBuilder *hitParams = [[GAIDictionaryBuilder alloc] init];

// Set campaign data on the map, not the tracker directly because it only needs
// to be sent once.

[[hitParams setCampaignParametersFromUrl:urlString] build];

// Campaign source is the only required campaign field. If previous call did
// not set a campaign source, use the hostname as a referrer instead.

if(![hitParams valueForKey:kGAICampaignSource] && [url host].length !=0) {

// Set campaign data on the map, not the tracker.

[hitParams set:kGAICampaignMedium value:@"referrer"];
[hitParams set:kGAICampaignSource value:[url host]];
 }

[tracker send:[[[GAIDictionaryBuilder createAppView] setAll:hitParams] build]];
```

## APP TRAFFIC SOURCE ATTRIBUTION

When you finish the integration (either Android or iOS), you will be able to see the sources of your acquisition campaigns and subsequent app sessions. Awesome. However, there remains one important question: how does Google Analytics attribute a source to a session? There are four possible ways for a user to reach an app, but only two outcomes when it comes to the way the source attribution behaves.

- The user opens the app without clicking on an external link: the current session will be attributed to the original source.
- The user clicks on an external link that does not include the campaign parameters (explained in Step 3 in the previous section): the current session will be attributed to the original source.
- The user clicks on an external link that includes the campaign parameters but the SDK was not modified to capture those links (as explained in Step 4 in the previous section): the current session will be attributed to the original source.
- The user clicks on an external link that includes the campaign parameters and the SDK was modified to capture campaign information (as explained in Step 4 in the previous section): The original campaign values will be overwritten and the current session will be attributed to the new source.

In case the user downloads the app again, it will actually be a new user with a new client ID, so the new source will depend on whether there are campaign parameters and whether the SDK was modified to capture the campaign information.

# Analyzing Mobile Apps—The Full Customer Journey

Now that you have all the data coming in, you can start analyzing your users' interactions and extracting insights to drive your business forward. In the following examples, I use the Google Play reports for two main reasons: (1) I have a better Google Play dataset and (2) The Referral Flow report is available only for Google Play.

The setup you went through in the previous section will bring additional data to the following reports in your app analytics account:

- **Sources reports**: This set of reports will show you where users who downloaded, installed, and launched your app come from. It will also provide metrics about how they behave and interact with your app.
- **Google Play Referral Flow report**: This report will show you the flow from Google Play views to installations to app launches—the full cycle.

In the next sections, you learn more about each of the reports and how to use them.

## Sources Reports

As shown in Figure 4-7, the default app sources report includes a line chart showing the trend for the New Users metric; it also shows a list of all the Source/Medium pairs that brought traffic to your app, sorted by number of new users. If you are interested only in Google Play or iTunes, you will find out-of-the-box reports for each in the left navigation sidebar.

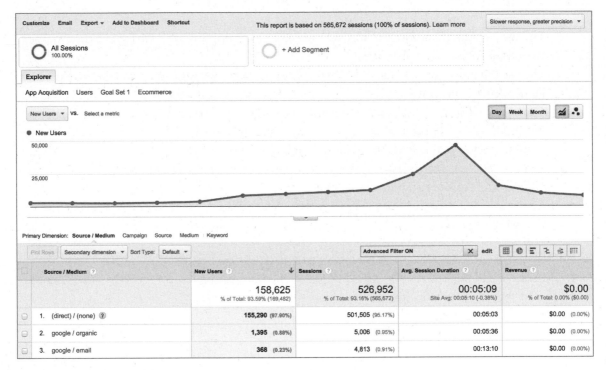

**Figure 4-7:** Default Sources report

The default Sources will show the App Acquisition trend in a glimpse. However, it is also possible to choose a different group of metrics to be shown by clicking on an item in the metric group selector (links beneath the Explorer tab in the report). Using those metrics, you will be able to pivot your analysis to see how traffic from each source engaged with the app. As you learned in Chapter 1, defining goals in your Google Analytics account is critical, and this report is one of the many that will provide great benefit when your goals are configured.

If you are interested in analyzing acquisition along with behavior and conversion data, I recommend creating a custom report using similar metrics/dimensions as the ones shown in

Figure 4-8. This example custom report can be imported to your account by following this link: `http://goo.gl/ptbQLb`.

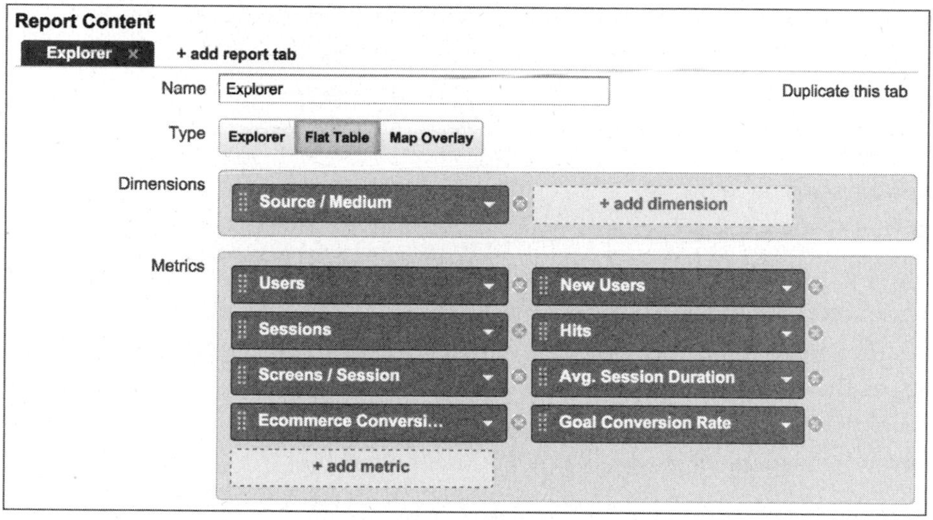

**Figure 4-8:** Acquisition, Behavior, and Conversion table

Figure 4-9 shows the Custom Report mentioned above in action. Here are a few topics you might want to focus on when looking at this table:

- **For each source**, examine the percentages inside the parentheses (columns 2–5) and compare them. If you notice big differences, it may be worth investigating further. For example, the source "google" (second row) represents 5.95% of all users who visited the app; however, it represents 6.45% of all new users, 7.54% of all sessions, and 8.71% of all hits. This means that, in this case, "google" is bringing users who are returning more often (higher percentage of sessions) and are more engaged (higher percentage of hits, which is the sum of all interactions in the app).
- **For each metric in columns 6–9**, compare all sources to understand how they differ in terms of engagement and conversions. For example, when comparing Goal Conversion Rate (last column) for all sources, you learn that "google" has a higher rate than all others in this table.

**NOTE** This report can be edited by clicking on Edit just below the report title. This might be important if your company uses a different set of metrics to analyze acquisition, behavior, and conversions.

| Source (?) | Users ↓ | New Users | Sessions | Hits | Screens / Session | Avg. Session Duration | Ecommerce Conversion Rate | Goal Conversion Rate |
|---|---|---|---|---|---|---|---|---|
| 1. (direct) | 193,735 (93.07%) | 166,115 (92.89%) | 503,029 (91.07%) | 3,547,812 (89.68%) | 3.17 | 00:04:43 | 0.00% | 83.03% |
| 2. google | 12,386 (5.95%) | 11,533 (6.45%) | 41,663 (7.54%) | 344,567 (8.71%) | 3.61 | 00:06:24 | 0.00% | 95.14% |
| 3. blogspot | 868 (0.42%) | 377 (0.21%) | 4,132 (0.75%) | 37,731 (0.95%) | 3.59 | 00:06:48 | 0.00% | 92.35% |
| 4. gplus | 383 (0.18%) | 312 (0.17%) | 1,322 (0.24%) | 10,319 (0.26%) | 3.53 | 00:05:58 | 0.00% | 93.27% |
| 5. twitter | 262 (0.13%) | 151 (0.08%) | 836 (0.15%) | 7,347 (0.19%) | 3.53 | 00:05:56 | 0.00% | 91.87% |

**Figure 4-9:** Analyzing Acquisition performance.

Another interesting way to analyze the data is to compare the performance of different mobile devices for each traffic source. In Figure 4-10 you will find such a comparison, where you can see the top three devices for traffic source "google" and how they compare to the average goal conversion rate of the app. In order to see the same report in your account, log in to your Google Analytics Account and find the Sources report under the Acquisition tab on the left sidebar; then click All and choose your settings based on the explanation below (also shown in Figure 4-10).

1. **Primary dimension:** The main dimension you want to analyze.
2. **Secondary dimension:** The dimension that will be used to segment your primary dimension.
3. **Filter:** Filters the table to show only one or more elements of the primary dimension.
4. **Chart Type:** There are several ways to visualize Google Analytics data; the visualization chosen in Figure 4-10 is the fourth icon starting from left, which is the Comparison chart.
5. **Sorting Metric:** Defines the order in which the primary dimension is sorted.
6. **Comparison Metric:** Defines which metric will be used to compare to the website average (the metrics available will depend on which metric group you have selected above the line chart).

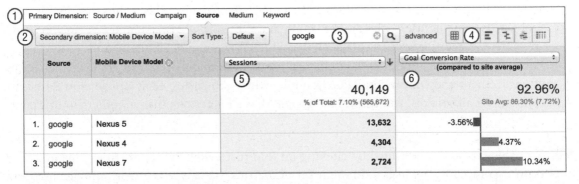

**Figure 4-10:** Comparing mobile device model performance

Note that this report can also be segmented using the Google Analytics segment builder, which means you can build custom segments to analyze your user acquisition in more detail. Learn more about segments in Google Analytics at `http://goo.gl/1IrUjV`.

# Google Play Referral Flow Report

The Google Play Referral Flow is an extremely insightful report in that it is the only way to see the full user journey, from the moment users see the app description on Google Play until the first time they open the app.

In Figure 4-11 you can see the default report, which includes a flow visualization on the top and a table in the bottom, both showing the same data. The visualization will help you understand the overall trend at a glimpse, while the table will help you drill down into the actual behavior by each source.

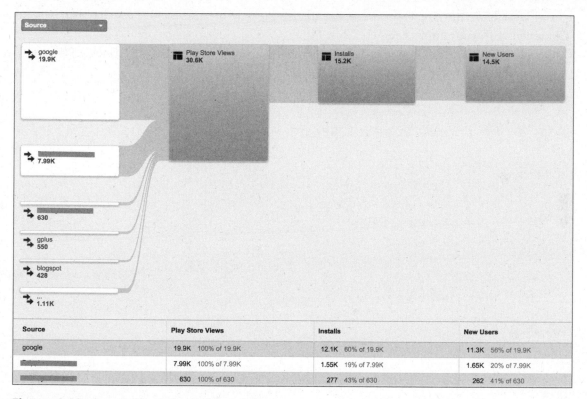

| Source | Play Store Views | | Installs | | New Users | |
|---|---|---|---|---|---|---|
| google | 19.9K | 100% of 19.9K | 12.1K | 60% of 19.9K | 11.3K | 56% of 19.9K |
| | 7.99K | 100% of 7.99K | 1.55K | 19% of 7.99K | 1.65K | 20% of 7.99K |
| | 630 | 100% of 630 | 277 | 43% of 630 | 262 | 41% of 630 |

**Figure 4-11:** Google Play Referral Flow report

A good way to use the table in Figure 4-10 is to look at the percentages in the parentheses and analyze their changes, both per row and per column:

- ■ **In-row analysis**: Analyzing the percentages of each step for every source will provide a quick funnel analysis showing which steps are not working for each of the sources.
- ■ **In-column analysis**: Comparing percentages for each of the columns will show which sources are performing the best for each of the steps.

## Summary

In this chapter you learned about the possible ways to bring Google Play and iTunes data into Google Analytics. As you have seen, the end result of the integrations will be a deeper understanding of acquisition campaigns (for both Google Play and iTunes) and the full customer journey (Google Play only). The reports that will show the data from the integrations are as follows:

- **Sources reports**: This set of reports will show you where users who downloaded, installed, and launched your app come from. It will also provide metrics about how they behave and interact with your app.
- **Google Play Referral Flow report**: This report will show you the flow from Google Play views to installations to app launches—the full cycle.

# 5 Webmaster Tools Integration

In order to provide helpful information for webmasters who want to optimize their website visibility on search results, Google created Webmaster Tools. These tools provide a wealth of information regarding Google organic search, including (but not limited to) crawling, indexing, traffic, and search appearance data.

If this is the first time you've read about Webmaster Tools, you should definitely get more involved with it, no matter if you are an analyst, a marketer, or a website owner. The rich data provided by the tools can help optimize your website visibility and usability in many ways. Read more about Webmaster Tools at `http://goo.gl/nEVgBM`.

This chapter provides a detailed step-by-step guide to integrating Webmaster Tools into Google Analytics as well as a walkthrough to the reports available once the integration is complete. While not all data can be imported from Webmaster Tools into Google Analytics, this integration will bring additional reports into Google Analytics, which can save time while analyzing Search Engine Optimization–related data.

## Linking Webmaster Tools to Google Analytics

The first step to linking a Webmaster Tools account to a Google Analytics property is having the right access levels. In order to link the accounts you must have Edit rights on Google Analytics and be an owner on the Webmaster Tools account of the site you want to import the data from. Learn more about access levels in both tools:

- **Google Analytics:** `http://goo.gl/G8dZnN`
- **Webmaster Tools:** `http://goo.gl/tOCNad`

It is also important to note that the accounts are linked on the Google Analytics property level; a website on Webmaster Tools can be linked to only one property on Google Analytics. And since the integration allows for just one-to-one linking, it might be affected by the way Google Analytics has been implemented.

For example, when measuring websites that span multiple top-level domains (such as `daniel.com`, `daniel.co.uk`, and `daniel.com.br`), a common solution for implementing Google Analytics is to have all top-level domains under the same property to make aggregation simpler. In that case, filters would be used to create a view for each domain. Since Webmaster Tools accept only one top-level domain per account, you would need to open one Webmaster Tools account for each top-level domain. In such circumstances it would be problematic to have the accounts linked properly, as you would have multiple Webmaster Tools accounts that relate to a single Google Analytics property.

**NOTE** If you are not acquainted with the Google Analytics hierarchy, read the following article to understand how accounts, properties, and views work: `http://goo.gl/TAv93N`.

If you have a Google Analytics property that relates to a single top-level domain and a Webmaster Tools account for this domain, the linking should be straightforward. First, log in to Google Analytics (make sure you have Edit permissions for the relevant property), and then click on the Admin link on the top of your screen.

You will reach your administrator panel. Click All Products under the Property Linking section. If this Google Analytics property is not linked to any Webmaster Tools account, you should see the snippet shown in Figure 5-1 when you scroll down that page.

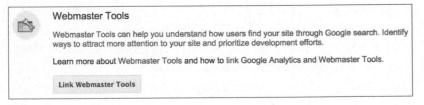

**Figure 5-1:** Linking Google Analytics and Webmaster Tools

In order to continue, you must be a Webmaster Tools owner in the account you want to link. Click on Link Webmaster Tools, and from the page displayed, click on Edit under the Webmaster Tools Settings section to reach the page shown in Figure 5-2 (in the Webmaster Tools website).

This page (see Figure 5-2) will list all accounts for which you are an owner. Choose the Webmaster Tools account you want to link to your Google Analytics property and click Save.

You will now be returned to the Google Analytics property settings page. Note that by default all views will show this Webmaster Tools account's data; if you want to limit the data to a number of views, click on the Enabled Views drop-down box and choose the views that should have this data enabled. Then click on Save.

Your Google Analytics account is now associated with your Webmaster Tools account. It's important to note that once the accounts are linked, the data from Webmaster Tools will populate Google Analytics reports retroactively, showing data starting from the day the Webmaster Tools account *or* the Google Analytics view was created, whichever came last.

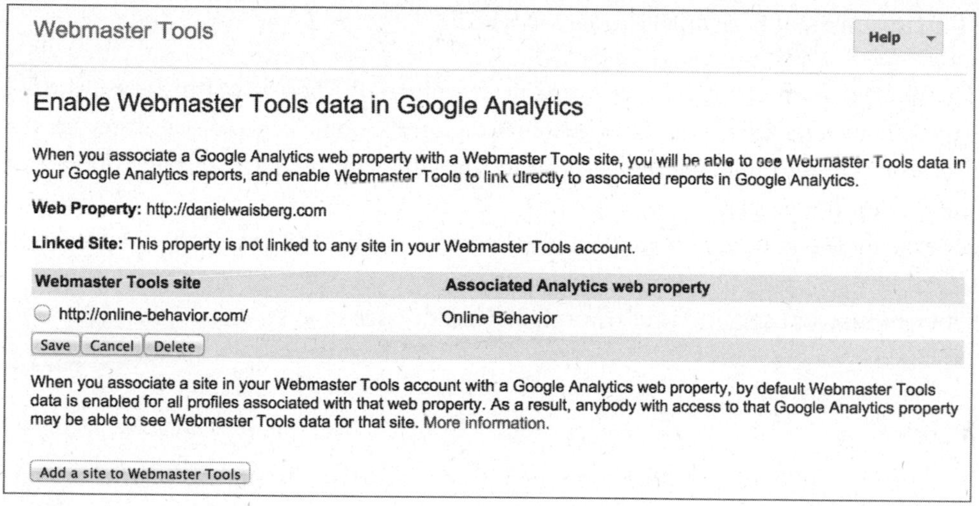

**Figure 5-2:** Enabling Webmaster Tools data in Google Analytics

In the next section, you learn more about the reports that are now available to you through Google Analytics.

# Analyzing Webmaster Tools Data on Google Analytics

In order to find the Webmaster Tools reports, called Search Engine Optimization, log into your Google Analytics account and look for them in the Acquisition tab (left sidebar) on the reporting interface. Three reports are available: Queries, Landing Pages, and Geographical Summary. In this section, you learn more about each report.

Note that the Google Analytics-Webmaster Tools integration is not as "deep" as the ones you've seen for AdWords and AdSense; it is not possible to analyze Webmaster Tools data using any other Google Analytics metric. For example, it would not be possible to segment queries by traffic source or any other metric unrelated to Webmaster Tools.

Once the accounts are linked, the following Google web search metrics will be available in the Search Engine Optimization reports:

- **Impressions:** The number of times a website URL appeared in Google organic search results.
- **Clicks:** The number of clicks on a website URL from a Google organic search result.
- **Average Position:** The average ranking of either a query or a landing page in Google organic search results. For example, if the query or landing page appeared at position 1 for one query and 3 for another query, the average position would be 2 ((1+3)/2). Keep in mind that if the site appeared several times for a specific query, only the top position contributes to the average position score.
- **CTR (Click-Through Rate):** Calculated as Clicks/Impressions * 100.

The following dimensions will be available to be analyzed:

- **Queries:** The queries users click in Google organic search results before visiting a website.
- **Landing Pages:** The pages users land on when clicking on a Google organic search result. It's important to note that multiple queries can lead to the same landing page and one query can lead to multiple landing pages.
- **Google Property:** A breakdown of search activity by web search, mobile search, video search, and image search.
- **Country:** The country of users, derived from their IP addresses.

## Queries Report

This report displays the top 1,000 daily queries with the following metrics: impressions, clicks, average position, and CTR. You can also use country and Google property as a primary or secondary dimension. The direct link to the report is `http://goo.gl/2cILOh`.

This report allows for an interesting analysis that can provide actionable insights. Figure 5-3 shows, at a glance, the clicks for each query as compared to the average number of clicks on your website queries (sorted by impressions). The central line in the chart represents the website average, and bars to the left of it show that the number of clicks was below the average, while bars to the right of it show that the number of clicks was above the average. You can see the queries with the highest number of impressions and their clicks as compared to the website average.

For example, in Figure 5-3, you see that the query *types of graphs* is well positioned when it comes to query impressions; however, this query is very ineffective when it comes to attracting people to click on it from Google organic search results.

| Query | Impressions ⬍ ↓ | Clicks ⬍ (compared to site average) |
|---|---|---|
| | **188,231**<br>% of Total: 23.53% (800,000) | **20,855**<br>% of Total: 59.59% (35,000) |
| tag manager | 15,000 | 15,541.72% |
| analytics definition | 5,500 | 5,276.84% |
| google analytics | 5,500 | 144.40% |
| types of graphs | 3,500 | -100.00% |
| what is analytics | 3,500 | 8,209.66% |

**Figure 5-3:** Queries report in Google Analytics

Figure 5-3 will uncover queries that are receiving high amounts of impressions on search results but are not succeeding in turning searchers into website users—that is, queries with a low CTR.

A good practice to improve queries' CTR is to customize your search snippet, which is the few lines of text that appear under every search result. The search snippet can be the user's first interaction with your website, and ultimately it will determine the click-through rate of visitors coming from Google organic search. The snippet is what you promise to your user; are you delivering it in the landing page? Learn more about ways to customize search snippets at `http://goo.gl/OYPZEO`.

In order to reach the report shown in Figure 5-3, follow these steps:

1. Open the Queries report (**go to** `http://goo.gl/2cILOh`).
2. Change the graph type to Comparison by clicking on the fourth icon to the right of the filter box, above the main table.
3. Change the right-most drop-down to Clicks (see the top-right drop-down in Figure 5-3).

Another interesting way to look at this data is to apply filters to see how different types of queries perform (the filter field is available right above the table). Here are a few query filter examples you might want to apply to your data:

- **Branded vs. non-branded:** This will provide a better understanding of how you can improve your organic search results for users who already know you (branded queries) as opposed to those who arrived using a general query (non-branded queries).
- **Product category:** If you sell products on your website, it is a good idea to see which product categories are performing well when it comes to organic search results.
- **Content section:** If you have different content sections on your website, such as Men and Women for ecommerce websites or News and Travel for publishers, you might want to analyze queries related to each section separately.

## Landing Pages

This report shows the top 1,000 daily landing pages for users coming from Google organic search. The URLs are ranked by impressions (the number of times an organic search result included a snippet leading to the specific landing page) on Google search result pages. You see the number of impressions, clicks, average position, and CTR for your top 1,000 pages.

With this report, you can see which pages drive the most organic search traffic to your site and which pages might need content improvements in order to deliver a better click-through rate. The direct link to this report is `http://goo.gl/uH1Zvd`.

When discussing paid search campaigns, it is very natural to talk about landing page optimization; however, optimizing organic search landing pages is not so common. But the importance is the same; both should be highly efficient in engaging incoming traffic. As I previously mentioned, it is not possible to mix the metrics from Webmaster Tools with the standard Google Analytics metrics, which means you can't add a success metric to this report (such as ecommerce conversion rate). This means that you can only learn which page brings the highest number of organic sessions, but not its success.

You can tell from Figure 5-4 that the page with the highest number of impressions is /analytics/ google-tag-manager, but it has an average CTR of 3.33%. On the other hand, /analytics/filters has significantly fewer impressions but a much higher CTR of 6.11%, so it is probably doing a better job with the search snippet.

| Landing Page | Impressions ⓘ | ↓ Clicks ⓘ | Average Position ⓘ | CTR ⓘ |
|---|---|---|---|---|
| | **2,032,471** <br> % of Total: 112.92% (1,800,000) | **98,168** <br> % of Total: 109.08% (90,000) | **44** <br> % of Total: 88.56% (49) | **4.83%** <br> Site Avg: 5.00% (-3.40%) |
| 1. http://online-behavior.com/analytics/google-tag-manager | **450,000** (22.14%) | 15,000 (15.28%) | 5.3 (10.12%) | 3.33% |
| 2. http://online-behavior.com/analytics/chart-types | **170,000** (8.36%) | 4,500 (4.58%) | 73 (168.38%) | 2.65% |
| 3. http://online-behavior.com/analytics/demographics | **110,000** (5.41%) | 5,500 (5.60%) | 44 (100.63%) | 5.00% |
| 4. http://online-behavior.com/analytics/data-visualization | **90,000** (4.43%) | 2,000 (2.04%) | 130 (308.55%) | 2.22% |
| 5. http://online-behavior.com/analytics/filters | **90,000** (4.43%) | 5,500 (5.60%) | 16 (34.97%) | 6.11% |

**Figure 5-4:** Landing page report in Google Analytics

You can go one step further to understand landing pages performance by adding a secondary dimension to this report, as shown on Figure 5-5. The following link will lead you directly to the report: http://goo.gl/W8IGQV. I have highlighted all the Google image results in the Top 10 organic landing pages in Figure 5-5. As you can see, this instantly shows that while Google image is showing a large amount of impressions for these pages, the CTRs are significantly lower than those for Google web results.

| Landing Page | Google Property ⓘ | Impressions ⓘ | ↓ Clicks ⓘ | Average Position ⓘ | CTR ⓘ |
|---|---|---|---|---|---|
| | | **771,706** <br> % of Total: 96.46% (800,000) | **37,812** <br> % of Total: 94.53% (40,000) | **40** <br> % of Total: 103.67% (39) | **4.90%** <br> Site Avg: 5.00% (-2.00%) |
| 1. http://online-behavior.com/analytics/google-tag-manager | Web | **140,000** (18.14%) | 4,500 (11.90%) | 4.6 (9.08%) | 3.21% |
| 2. http://online-behavior.com/analytics/chart-types | Image | **50,000** (6.48%) | 1,300 (3.44%) | 77 (192.00%) | 2.60% |
| 3. http://online-behavior.com/analytics/demographics | Web | **40,000** (5.18%) | 2,000 (5.29%) | 19 (44.85%) | 5.00% |
| 4. http://online-behavior.com/analytics/filters | Web | **35,000** (4.54%) | 2,000 (5.29%) | 14 (32.07%) | 5.71% |
| 5. http://online-behavior.com/testing/content-experiments | Web | **35,000** (4.54%) | 1,600 (4.23%) | 16 (38.06%) | 4.57% |
| 6. http://online-behavior.com/analytics/dashboards | Web | **27,000** (3.50%) | 1,300 (3.44%) | 16 (37.82%) | 4.81% |
| 7. http://online-behavior.com/analytics/data-visualization | Image | **27,000** (3.50%) | 400 (1.06%) | 160 (404.52%) | 1.48% |
| 8. http://online-behavior.com/analytics/multi-channel-funnels | Web | **22,000** (2.85%) | 900 (2.38%) | 14 (31.91%) | 4.09% |
| 9. http://online-behavior.com/cartoons/inspiration | Image | **22,000** (2.85%) | 200 (0.53%) | 61 (153.31%) | 0.91% |
| 10. http://online-behavior.com/analytics/custom-variables-segmentation | Web | **18,000** (2.33%) | 1,000 (2.64%) | 10 (23.69%) | 5.56% |

**Figure 5-5:** Landing page report segmented by Google property

In addition to this initial segmentation, which is possible only in the Search Engine Optimization reports, there is a way to analyze organic traffic success using Google Analytics standard reports.

Next, you will learn how to analyze landing pages from organic search traffic and discover how well they are performing. You will not be able to see this analysis side by side with the Webmaster Tools metrics (impressions, clicks, average position, and CTR), but knowing organic landing page conversion rates will provide an excellent proxy for Search Engine Optimization success.

To perform this analysis, visit the standard Landing Pages report (direct link: `http://goo.gl/WQAi4x`), click on the box marked as letter A on Figure 5-6, and then choose Organic Traffic. (By default, your screen will show All Traffic instead of Organic Traffic.) You can also remove the All Traffic segment by clicking on the arrow on the upper-right corner of the box. Following this step, choose the visualization type Comparison—marked as letter C in Figure 5-6. Finally, choose the metric you would like to use as a comparison point just below the icons for visualization type. Note that you can also choose different metrics by choosing a different Metric group, as explained below.

The report shows all the landing pages from organic traffic and their performance when it comes to bounce rates and goals you have configured in your account.

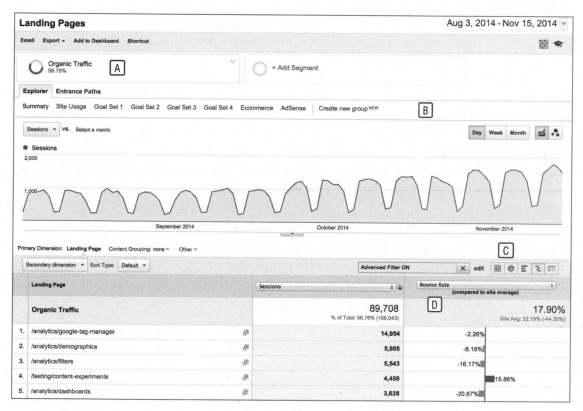

**Figure 5-6:** Analyzing organic landing pages in Google Analytics

Here is a quick explanation of what you see in Figure 5-6:

A. **Organic traffic segment:** This segment ensures that only organic search traffic information will appear in this report. If you want to learn more about segments, read `http://goo.gl/ZaG64q`.

B. **Metric group:** Each of the links represents a group of metrics to be displayed on the table. You will be able to see landing page performance by any goal set, ecommerce, AdSense revenue, or a customized set.

C. **Visualization type:** As you saw in the previous section, the Comparison visualization is very effective when analyzing data; it shows how each row compares to the average of the website for a specific metric (middle grey line). Note that for bounce rates (the rate at which visitors leave a website without interacting with it), lower is better; therefore a higher than average bar will be red and a lower than average bar is green. When you're looking at metrics such as conversion rates, the colors will be inversed.

D. **Metrics drop-down:** This drop-down can be used to choose which metric will be shown in the visualization. Metrics that can be used are % new visits, bounce rate, pages/visit, average visit duration, and other goal-conversion metrics.

If you analyze Figure 5-6, you can see that the website has a steady organic traffic growth. Looking at the Top 5 organic search landing pages shown in the table below the chart, you learn that besides number 4 they all have a lower than average bounce rate, which is a good sign. I also recommend that you change the metric group to check how landing pages perform for more meaningful metrics such as goal and ecommerce conversion rates. You might want to take further action on landing page number 4, `/testing/content-experiments`, probably by adding more engaging content and testing it through an A/B test.

I also highly recommend that you perform this analysis separately for organic search mobile traffic; this will give you an indication of how you are performing on mobile as well. In order to do that, add a mobile organic segment to your account using this link: `http://goo.gl/9sh2i8`. Then change the segment in the report shown in Figure 5-6 by clicking on Add Segment next to annotation A. Make sure to check the Webmaster Tools list of recommendations to optimize websites for mobile devices at `http://goo.gl/BMieZI`.

## Geographical Summary

The SEO Geographical Summary table provides a breakdown of impressions, clicks, and CTR with country as the default primary dimension. You can also select Google Property as a primary dimension to get a breakdown of the metrics by one of the following search types: web, image, mobile, mobile smartphone, or video. The direct link to this report is `http://goo.gl/6aaHrT`.

The default view in this report, which shows countries where your site has been exposed on search queries, will help you understand in which countries you appear the most on search results.

This view can be used to understand CTR from different countries, which might be used to decide which countries need their own localized version using the country language.

The second view provides information about Google search properties (image, web, mobile, video, and so on). In order to reach this view, visit the Geographical Summary default report and click on Google Property, as shown in Figure 5-7.

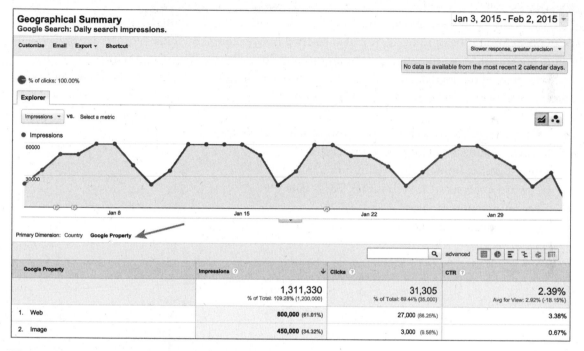

**Figure 5-7:** Finding the Google Property report

You can use the information in this view to understand how your site is optimized for different properties. For instance, based on the information shown in Figure 5-8, you might decide to try to optimize your search results on Google Image, which has a high number of impressions but a very low CTR.

| Google Property | Impressions ? | Clicks ? | CTR ? |
|---|---|---|---|
|  | 4,578,070<br>% of Total: 91.56% (5,000,000) | 96,010<br>% of Total: 106.68% (90,000) | 2.10%<br>Site Avg: 1.80% (16.51%) |
| 1. Web | 2,200,000 (48.06%) | 75,000 (78.12%) | 3.41% |
| 2. Image | 2,200,000 (48.06%) | 18,000 (18.75%) | 0.82% |
| 3. Mobile (smartphone) | 170,000 (3.71%) | 3,000 (3.12%) | 1.76% |
| 4. Unknown | 8,000 (0.17%) | 5 (0.01%) | 0.06% |
| 5. Video | 70 (0.00%) | 5 (0.01%) | 7.14% |

**Figure 5-8:** Google properties report in Google Analytics

## Summary

In this chapter you learned how to link Google Analytics and Webmaster Tools accounts. As you saw, while this integration is not as robust as the AdWords and AdSense integrations, it is certainly helpful and can be used to extract important insights.

You learned some techniques to help analyze the new data. You saw how to uncover low-performance queries by looking at click-through rates from Google organic search results and learned why organic landing pages should be optimized. You also learned how to compare query performance by Google search property and how to optimize it by improving your organic search snippets.

To learn more about analysis techniques for performing Search Engine Optimization using Google Analytics, read `http://goo.gl/rrPRVV`. Here are the techniques discussed in that article:

- Landing page analysis that focuses on Google/organic traffic
- Segment analysis of Google/organic traffic
- Multi-channel funnels and attribution analysis
- Keyword analysis with Webmaster Tools data
- Generating content ideas
- Internal site search analysis

# 6

# YouTube Integration

In this chapter, you learn about the integration between Google Analytics and YouTube, which is an important platform for video content publishers. This integration allows you to understand how users interact with your YouTube channel using Google Analytics reports.

Although the official integration does not provide data usage information per video, in this chapter you learn a custom way to bring data related to interactions with videos embedded on your website. The solution in the second section of the chapter was contributed by Stéphane Hamel.

## Integrating YouTube Into Google Analytics

The integration between Google Analytics and YouTube is very straightforward. Sign in to your YouTube account and visit http://goo.gl/zzmtwh. On that page you will find a box where you can enter your Google Analytics property tracking ID, similar to Figure 6-1.

**Figure 6-1:** Inserting the Google Analytics tracking code into a YouTube channel

As you can see, it is a very simple interface. The only required step is to add the Google Analytics property tracking ID you use to track your website, or a new one especially for YouTube. There are two ways to set up this integration:

- **Using the same property ID**: The advantage of this option is to see a summary of all sessions to your properties; however, it is not possible to deduplicate users visiting both the channel and your website.
- **Using a separate property ID**: The advantage of this option is its simplicity; no filters or views are required. You will see the reports for the website and YouTube channel on its own Google Analytics property.

Once this step is completed, your Google Analytics account will start gathering information about activity on the YouTube channel.

**NOTE** *It is important to note that this integration provides data only about the channel page; it does not provide information about activity on individual video pages.* Read more about individual video interactions at the end of this section. Also learn how to measure interaction in an embedded YouTube player on your website in the contribution written by Stephane Hamel at the end of the chapter.

Next, I go over the settings that should be implemented in case you choose to track your YouTube channel using the same Google Analytics property ID as the one you use for your main site. In this case, I recommend creating YouTube and non-YouTube views in Google Analytics. Create new views with the filters shown in Figures 6-2 and 6-3 (one view for each filter) on your account. To learn more about creating views, visit `http://goo.gl/eevIxD`; to learn more about creating filters, visit `http://goo.gl/T9hjmV`.

- **Only YouTube Traffic**: This view shows only the behavior of users in the YouTube channel. Use the filter in Figure 6-2 for this view.
- **NO YouTube Traffic**: This view shows only the behavior of users to the website. Use the filter in Figure 6-3 for this view.

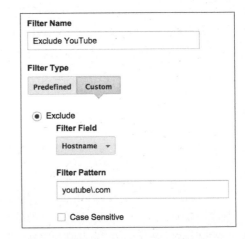

**Figure 6-2:** Filter to include YouTube traffic    **Figure 6-3:** Filter to exclude YouTube traffic

In addition to the preceding views, be sure to have an overall view that includes all domains. This will help you analyze the aggregate traffic to the website and to the YouTube brand channel.

Integrating Google Analytics with YouTube will allow you to see which videos, and which annotations inside those videos, bring users to the channel page. This can provide insights into which videos are driving users to further interactions with your channel. In order to find this information, visit the All Pages report at `http://goo.gl/BKU8LK` in the Only YouTube Traffic view. On this report you will find URLs such as the following: `/profile?annotation_id=annotation_1691&feature=iv` `&user=onbehavior&src_vid=cstxyj0tj6g`.

As you can see, those views of your profile (or channel) carry parameters that tell you the `annotation_id` and `src_vid` (source video). This can be used to analyze annotations success in bringing video watchers into your company channel, exposing him/her to other videos from your brand channel.

If you want a more in-depth analysis of your video interactions as well as your watchers audience, YouTube provides a rich Analytics tool for video creators at `http://goo.gl/1FuYlj`. The following list explains some of the information you will find in the tool. The metrics can be segmented by individual video or playlist or seen in total; they can also be segmented by country and viewed for any specific date range.

- Performance
    - Video views
    - Estimated minutes watched
    - Estimated earnings
- Engagement
    - Likes
    - Dislikes
    - Comments
    - Shares
    - Favorites added
    - Subscribers
    - Average view duration
    - Average percentage viewed
- Demographics
    - Gender
    - Age
- Devices
    - Device type
    - Operating system
- Traffic Sources

# YouTube Video Tracking in Google Analytics Using Google Tag Manager

*This section was contributed by Stéphane Hamel, a freelance consultant in the field of Digital Analytics. Named Most Influential Contributor by the Digital Analytics Association, he is the creator of the Online Analytics Maturity Model and the Web Analytics Solution Profiler.*

This guide will empower you to start measuring user interactions with embedded videos on your website. After you finish this implementation, visit the Top Events report at `http://goo.gl/EIbyDK` and you will find the following event hierarchy:

- Event category: video
- Event actions: play, pause, exit, 0%, 25%, 50%, 75% and 100%
- Event label: video unique identifier and title

## Implementation Details

This example uses the YouTube JavaScript API (`http://goo.gl/mgi4WR`) to expose user interactions with the video. In order for this to work, each of your YouTube embeds needs to include `enable-jsapi=1` in the link of the video—for example (bold code below):

```
<iframe width="420" height="315"
  src="//www.youtube.com/embed/RvwOuxuYBCo?enablejsapi=1"
  frameborder="0" allowfullscreen></iframe>
```

**NOTE** The `Is YouTube Present` variable (discussed later in this section) could be modified to automatically add `enablejsapi` if it's not there, but this will result in a quick flash of the YouTube frame.

In order to implement this solution, you need to use some built-in variables and create a couple of user-defined variables, two tags, and two triggers. If you are not acquainted with those definitions, read through `http://goo.gl/c4rP83`.

The actual definitions of the elements mentioned in the previous paragraph are lengthy and include long pieces of code, so you will find all of them in a JSON file available for download at `http://goo.gl/rjP3ar`.

Google Tag Manager allows users to import and merge container settings to your existing container through a simple process using JSON files. In order to implement this solution, visit the link in the previous paragraph and download the file to your computer. Then log in to your Google Tag Manager account and choose the container you would like to use for this solution.

As shown in Figure 6-4, once you choose your account and container, click on Admin and then on Import Container.

Once you start the Container Import process, you will see a screen similar to Figure 6-5. In this page you will be given the option to upload the file you downloaded in the previous step. You will also be able to choose between "Overwrite" and "Merge" with the existing container. In this case it is recommended that you choose "Merge" and then "Rename conflicting tags, triggers, and variables." This option will be safer, as it avoids losing any previous configurations; you can always revisit your account and delete tags, triggers, and variables if they are not being used.

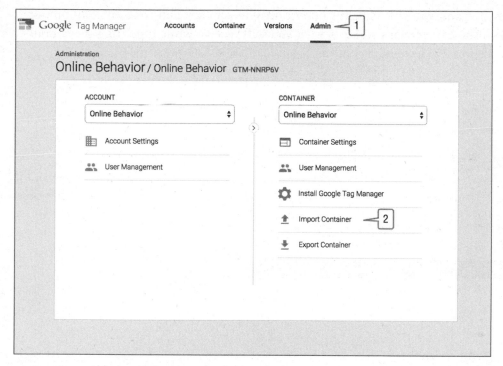

**Figure 6-4:** Google Tag Manager settings interface

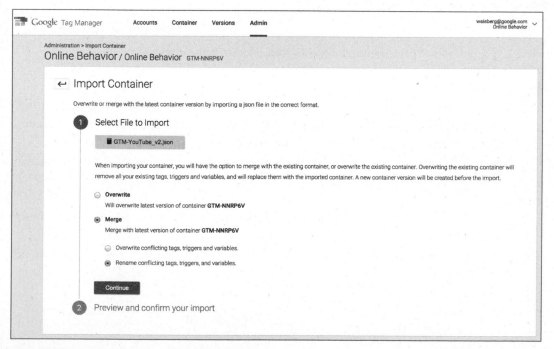

**Figure 6-5:** Importing and merging the container

Click on Continue and you will have the opportunity to preview and confirm your container import. Figure 6-6 shows a screen similar to what you will receive while importing the container provided in this section. Review it and confirm.

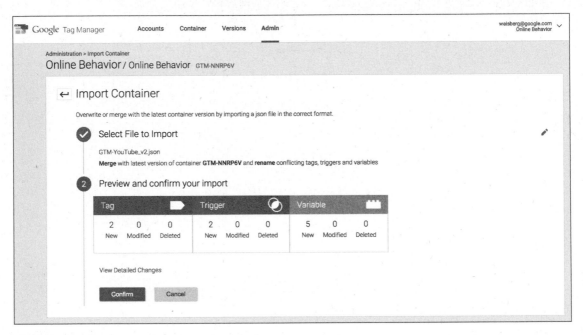

**Figure 6-6:** Preview and confirm your container import

Following is a quick description of the elements imported to your container:

- **Tags**
  - YouTube Listener contains the custom logic to detect player events exposed through the YouTube JavaScript API. When a valid event is detected, relevant information is pushed into the dataLayer and a custom event is set to youtube.
  - YouTube Events is a standard Universal Analytics event triggered by the custom dataLayer event mentioned above.
- **Triggers**
  - YouTube Ready is a trigger initiated when at least one YouTube embedded video is found and the API is ready.
  - YouTube Event is triggered when a relevant activity is detected by the custom YouTube Listener.

- **Variables**
  - `Is YouTube Present` returns `true` if there is at least one embedded YouTube video on the page.
  - `Data Layer Action` and `Label` retrieve the values exposed by the custom listener.

## Custom Report to Monitor Video Performance

That's it! Now you can track YouTube-embedded video on your own website thanks to Google Tag Manager and Universal Analytics. If you want to get details about how individual videos are performing, follow these steps:

1. Visit the Top Events report at `http://goo.gl/EIbyDK` and click on Video.
2. Click on Customize on the top of the report.
3. Under Dimension Drilldowns, remove the Event Category dimension and switch Event Action with Event Label. It should then read Event Label/Event Action.
4. Modify the filter to read "Event Category Equals Video" so that only videos are shown in this new custom report.

Voilà! You now have detailed performance info about each video embedded on your website.

## Summary

In this chapter you learned about the YouTube integration, which is not as tight as the AdWords or AdSense integrations but provides valuable information about channel page behavior and annotation success.

You also learned how to analyze video interactions on embedded players on your website using a custom container that can be imported to your Google Tag Manager account. This solution will provide you with information on interactions such as play and pause, as well as the percentage watched and for which embedded video.

# Custom
# Integrations

# 7 Custom Data Integration

*This chapter was contributed by Corey L. Koberg, Founder and Senior Partner at Cardinal Path, where he leads the data science, analysis, and product development teams. He is a well-known speaker, having keynoted and led sessions on advertising, analytics, and optimization at conferences and events across the globe. He has consulted for dozens of Fortune 500 companies, such as Google, Chevron, NBC, Papa John's, National Geographic, Time Warner, Universal Music, DeVry University, and others, to improve the effectiveness of their digital presence through results-oriented, data-driven optimization.*

During Google Analytics' first few years there was really only one way to get data into it: the JavaScript tracking code that was embedded into website HTML. Additional data could be included with the data sent back to Google Analytics, such as a custom variable, campaign information, or transaction results. With time, Google Analytics has become a much more versatile platform that accepts data in four primary ways:

- JavaScript tracking code for websites
- Mobile SDK for apps
- Measurement Protocol for hits from anywhere (such as a point of sale)
- Data Import for enhancing data (CSV uploads)

## Methods to Import Data into Google Analytics

The first three of the preceding methods generate new data. For example, a new user to a website initiates a session that sends data to Google Analytics via a JavaScript tag on the page. The Universal Analytics tracking script is extremely versatile and comprehensive. However, the Mobile App SDK and the Measurement Protocol are both important additions to an analytics toolkit as businesses try to capture all customer touch points—websites, mobile apps, and even offline elements such as point-of-sale terminals.

But despite sending data to Google Analytics, both the JavaScript and the SDKs are not what you might consider a data import; they are the most common ways to track online behavior and send it back to Google Analytics. In this section, you learn more about two ways to import additional data into Google Analytics: the Measurement Protocol and the Data Import. Following this overview, you'll see a few common examples of exactly how to conduct the import.

## The Measurement Protocol

When you think about "importing" data into Google Analytics that you want to analyze, you are likely thinking about data related to events and interactions that you have stored elsewhere (perhaps in a spreadsheet or database) and want to upload to Google Analytics, even if those interactions happened in the past.

The Measurement Protocol is a completely flexible method for sending that data to Google Analytics directly, without the need to use JavaScript, SDK, or any other collection mechanism. All you have to do is format the data in the proper way (a simple HTTP `GET` or `POST` request), and Google will accept and process the data. Google will even join that data to existing sessions and backdate it if they receive it soon enough (within four hours of the event).

While the flexibility of the Measurement Protocol means that you can now theoretically send data to Google Analytics from theme park turnstiles, airplane transponders, and other "sensor data," the most common use cases still involve digital marketing. For example, if a customer clicks on an ad and receives a quote online, but completes the purchase in a call center, that revenue (and attribution credit for the ad) would normally go untracked. However, if the call center software was to send the conversion data back to Google Analytics, the revenue would be tracked and potentially even connected all the way back to the original ad that drove the purchase.

A similar scenario unfolds when free trials automatically roll over into paid accounts if not canceled by a certain date. Normally that "conversion" would happen behind the scenes in the back-office order processing software and Google Analytics would never be able to distinguish between which visitors (and which marketing campaigns) canceled their trials and which ones went on to convert into customers. Using the Measurement Protocol, that software could process a report each night that sends the conversion data back to Google Analytics identifying which of the trials converted, as well as any auto renewals that may take place.

Point-of-sale systems that process in-store pickup of online orders, coupon redemptions, and repeat purchases where the original purchase was online but follow-ups occurred offline are all common use cases that show the versatility of the Measurement Protocol. To learn more about the exact format required by the Measurement Protocol, see the Developer's Guide at `http://goo.gl/5VfF9k`.

> **NOTE** See Chapter 8, "User Data Integration," for a detailed example of how to use the Measurement Protocol to integrate customer usage behavior data across devices into Google Analytics.

## Data Import

While the Measurement Protocol contains entirely new interaction hits that may be joined with existing sessions or start entirely new ones, some of the data you'll import to Google Analytics is specifically designed to supplement existing hits and simply provide more context.

For example, a news publisher might want to classify and analyze the content on the site by the page author and category in order to determine the most popular authors and topics. That data can be uploaded to Google Analytics via a spreadsheet and associated with those pages using the page URL as the key that links the existing data with the new, as shown in Figure 7-1. This is known as "widening" the existing dimensions to include new data fields, known as *dimensions*, that are now associated with the original data. That's why a previous version of this feature was called "dimension widening."

| utm_source | utm_medium | City | Pageviews | Page URL | | Page URL | Author | Category |
|---|---|---|---|---|---|---|---|---|
| newsletter | email | London | 3 | /bigquery.php | ⟷ | /bigquery.php | Ckoberg | bigdata |

**Figure 7-1:** Widening the page URL dimension using Data Import

## Advantages of Data Import

Here are some of the most prominent advantages of using Data Import:

- **No code to write, maintain, or publish:** A site owner could potentially include the author and category data in the previous example as Custom Dimensions sent back to Google Analytics included with the initial pageview tracking. However, this would require the tracking code on the site to be modified, which in many organizations can be a long and arduous process.
- **Data may not be available before the pageview hit is sent:** In order to send the data to Google Analytics with the pageview, the information must be available at the time the pageview hit is sent, which is usually immediately upon page load. Oftentimes, the kinds of data you'll want to supplement with is either not available to the web server (back-office and CRM data) or simply hasn't happened yet (delayed conversions and refunds).
- **Data may be confidential:** Anything sent with the hit itself can be seen in plain text, but some information that is useful for analysis may be too confidential to display publicly. For example, perhaps you are analyzing results of a new page layout and want to understand not only the revenue and quantity of items sold, but also the margin and profitability of each item. While gross revenue is obvious to the purchaser (they know what they paid!), the profit margin is likely a confidential value and is better uploaded securely after the fact.
- **Can accommodate larger sizes:** If the data is uploaded via Data Import rather than as part of the pageview, it avoids the size limitations that exist regarding what can be sent via the client's browser and also reduces the burden on their Internet connection.

## Data Types and Use Cases

There are lots of business uses for Data Import, but they tend to fall into a few categories, some of which have specific formats and processes for uploading to Google. The following sections explain several examples.

**Campaign Data**   Normally with Google Analytics, you use campaign tagging to include information about the source, medium, campaign, and even ad creative and keywords by individual query string parameters, such as this:

```
http://cardinalpath.com/?utm_source=newsletter&utm_medium=email&utm_
content=button2&utm_campaign=sitelaunch
```

But that long URL may pass information you don't want to reveal, requires Google-specific formatting, and is limited to a few dimension types. Many systems, such as marketing automation and ad networks, utilize a single campaign ID, which you can now expand to the full dataset via Data Import. An example of the previous URL formatted to utilize this single parameter campaign tracking may look like this:

```
http://cardinalpath.com/?utm_id=4567
```

**NOTE**   You can find a step-by-step guide showing how to import campaign data to your Property at http://goo.gl/yYneir.

**CRM Data**   Many companies have a wealth of customer data that can be highly illuminating when merged with online behavior data, such as what you would get from Google Analytics.

For example, a newspaper may want to indicate whether users are subscribers, if they subscribe to print and digital, how long they have been a subscriber, and so on. Another company may have already classified its customers into "high-value prospects" and want to confidentially add those fields to the customer record to enable that group to be analyzed. Lifetime value (LTV) calculations are often kept in CRMs and can be useful to import and attach to user records for analysis. Perhaps your company divides geographies into sales regions, such as "Southern Europe," and wants to do analysis on performance for each region. B2B companies may classify visitors by their organization size (SMB versus enterprise) so they can understand how each consumes their site content.

The examples are endless and there is often a high business value for integrating this data. You learn more about this use case in Chapter 8, which deals specifically with user data integration.

Be sure to avoid pulling in names, phone numbers, emails, social security numbers, or any other personally identifiable information (PII).

**NOTE**   You can find a step-by-step guide showing how to import user data to your Property at http://goo.gl/Glzg7c.

**URLs and Query String Parameters**   The initial example in this chapter pointed out that pages (identified by their unique URLs) may have other metadata—such as author, category, and section—that is useful for analysis. But if your site has a clear URL structure with logical subdirectories or utilizes query string variables to hold information that can be used for analysis, you can parse that data from the URL and include it as a dimension along with the pageview. You will find a step-by-step guide on how to perform this integration in the following examples.

**Transactions**   When a transaction takes place, there are many opportunities to supplement this data. Previously, we discussed adding margin data to products or transactions, but you could also include additional category information, suppliers, and cart options such as in-store pickup. You can also more accurately measure revenue by tracking refunds associated with transactions to get a true accounting of site, audience, product, and campaign performance.

> **NOTE**   You can find a step-by-step guide showing how to import refund data to your Property at `http://goo.gl/1whJbe`.

**Cost Data for Marketing Campaigns**   Google AdWords, DoubleClick, AdSense, and other Google properties easily integrate critical ad performance data, such as cost, clicks, and impressions, into Google Analytics. Utilizing the Cost Data Import feature, you can now upload this critical data from non-Google sources. You learn more about this use case in Chapter 9, which deals specifically with marketing campaign data integration.

**Custom Data**   The previous sections have outlined some common examples, but you are not limited to them. Google allows you to widen dozens of the data dimensions flowing into Google Analytics automatically, as well as the Custom Dimensions that you add to your site.

> **NOTE**   You can find a step-by-step guide showing how to import Custom Data to your Property at `http://goo.gl/w7nxXj`.

# Real-World Examples

While the process of importing data is relatively straightforward, there are a few best practices and pitfalls you'll want to avoid. This section walks you through a few examples to show you exactly how to proceed.

## Importing Content Data

The example shown previously in Figure 7-1 is useful for illustration purposes because it's easy to understand how the key joins those two items. But in the real world, this rarely works out so easily. Even if you did have only nice, clean URLs, you would have to upload a dataset for each new page published on the site. Most sites that are interested in analyzing author and content categories are updated frequently and would have to manually upload a new spreadsheet each time an article is published, which is often untenable.

If the only option is to match each specific URL on a 1:1 basis with the imported data, the Data Import feature available through the Management API can automate the upload process. But even then, you'll want to be careful that a single page isn't represented by multiple URLs. For example, the content on the page:

```
/blog/bigquery.php
```

May also be returned by URLs such as:

```
/blog/bigquery.php?char=utf-8
/blog/bigquery.php?char=utf-8&lang=EN
/blog/bigquery.php?affiliate=cj345&emailID=7893
```

In that case, you should utilize Regular Expression (RegEx) pattern matching to look specifically for the part of the URL that indicates the information and avoid the often useless info at the end. In the previous example, the RegEx pattern you would use is as follows:

```
/blog/([^/]+).php
```

This pattern matches just the initial part of the URL and ignores the trailing parameters. A strategy using automated API uploads and RegEx pattern checking would be far more efficient and robust than manual imports.

But there may be a simpler way, as many Content Management Systems include data in the query string parameters of the URL. For example, if the previous URLs were written as:

```
/blog/bigquery.php?char=utf-8&lang=EN&author=CKoberg&cat=bigdata
```

You could ignore the format of the URL, avoid any regular expression pattern matching, and simply tell Google Analytics to populate the dimensions from the parameters author and cat. You can learn how to do this in the following step-by-step guide.

### Step 1: Create the Custom Dimension Data Fields that Will Hold the New Data

In this case, you might call them authorID and catID. This is done via the Admin section on Google Analytics by clicking on Custom Definitions and then Custom Dimensions. Check out this guide from the Help Center: http://goo.gl/dLHx3a.

### Step 2: Choose the Dataset Type

From the Admin section, under the Property menu, select Data Import, then + New Data Set, and then for this example choose Content Data, as shown in Figure 7-2.

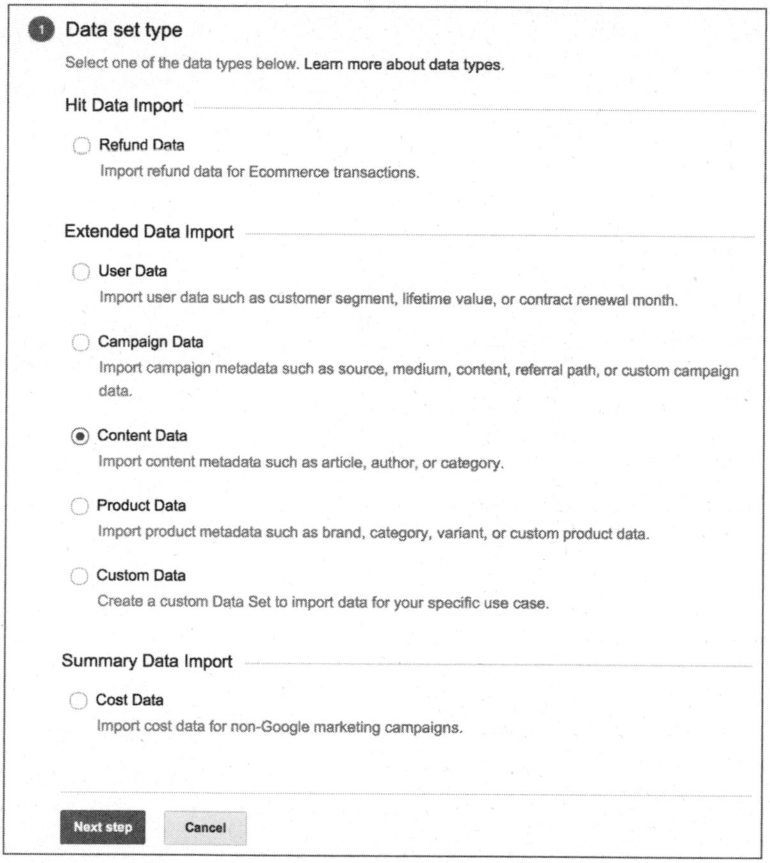

**Figure 7-2:** Choosing the dataset type for Data Import

## Step 3: Provide the Dataset Details

Choose an easily recognizable and logical name, such as `AuthorID`, and select the views you want to associate with the data import, as shown in Figure 7-3. Note that you need to import `AuthorID` and `CatID` separately.

## Step 4: Create the Schema

This is a critical step where you tell Google Analytics which shared key will join the data (in this case, the Page dimension, which by default is set to the Page URL) and which Custom Dimension fields to map the new data into. In this example, you will specify not only that it is the URL, but specifically the query string parameter (see Figure 7-4). Click the Query Refinement link and enter `author` as the variable that will hold the value you're interested in matching. Next, select the Custom Dimension `AuthorID` as the field you want to populate with the data.

In this case, you aren't overwriting any data that would be part of the standard pageview, so the overwrite hit data option doesn't apply. Finally, select Save.

**Figure 7-3:** Naming the dataset and choosing availability across views

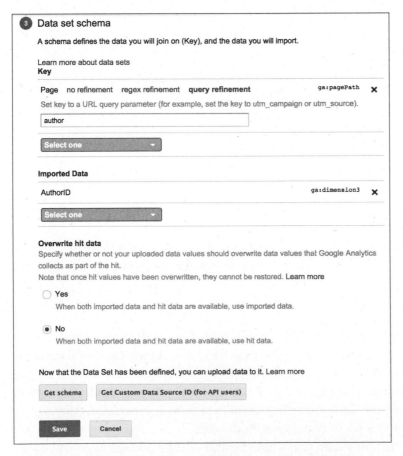

**Figure 7-4:** Creating the dataset schema to import custom data

## Step 5: Download the Schema

After saving the previous step, Google will prepare a CSV file that you will need to populate with your data to import. Click the Get Schema button (see the bottom of Figure 7-4) to download the specially formatted file. The file will be an empty CSV that simply has the key to match and Custom Dimensions that hold the imported data as the headings. In this case, the dimensions would be `ga:pagePath` and `ga:dimension1` (the number at the end depends on which Custom Dimension slot you are using).

## Step 6: Populate the CSV with the Data to Import

In this example, you need to specify the author names that correspond to each value, as shown in Figure 7-5. Note that although this example uses author names in both cases, it doesn't import the data from the query string or URL; it's simply using the data as a match to indicate which data should be populated. See the sample populated CSV in Figure 7-5.

| | A | B |
|---|---|---|
| 1 | ga:pagePath | ga:dimension1 |
| 2 | Koberg | CKoberg |
| 3 | Waisberg | DWaisberg |
| 4 | NM | NMihailovski |
| 5 | Cutroni | JCutroni |
| 6 | AL | ALangshur |

**Figure 7-5:** Sample populated CSV to upload

## Step 7: Upload the Data

Now that Google Analytics understands how to receive and process the data and you've populated the CSV file, it's time to upload the data. Click on Manage Uploads from the Data Import section (Figure 7-6) on the row that matches your new dataset and select your CSV file for upload. A progress bar will indicate upload status and whether your data file was imported successfully. Note that you may have to refresh the page.

| + NEW DATA SET | | Q Search | |
|---|---|---|---|
| **Name** | **Type** | **Data Set ID** | **Action** |
| AuthorID | Content Data | _nr1AOqRR-SalX-SyHi-Wg | Manage uploads |
| catID | Daily Upload | UeZ4U79cRnml3-842Zz9jQ | Manage uploads |

**Figure 7-6:** Uploading the data to Google Analytics

### Step 8: Create a Custom Report

That's it! Google Analytics now has your data and will join it with the pageview data. But since the data you uploaded is not part of the default Google Analytics dataset, there are no built-in reports that will display the data. Therefore, you will need to create a custom report by clicking Customization from the top navigation bar and then + New Custom Report, and then selecting your new Custom Dimensions along with any metrics you would like to analyze their performance by.

## Importing Product Profit Margin Data

You learned earlier in this section that understanding profit alongside quantity and revenue would be very useful, but likely confidential, so it makes a great use case for direct Data Import. In this case, you follow the same steps, with some slight variations. When you create the Custom Dimension to store the data, you select a Product Scope dimension instead, as shown in 7-7.

**Figure 7-7:** Creating a Product Scope custom dimension

The dataset schema will be similar, except you need to choose Product SKU as the key and the newly created Profit Margin dimension as the container, as shown in Figure 7-8.

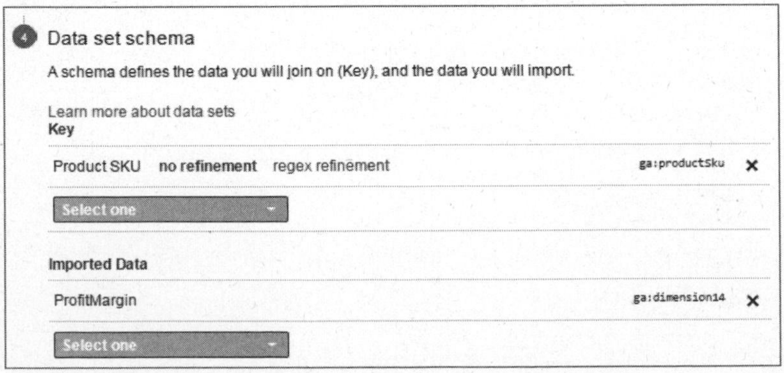

**Figure 7-8:** Defining the dataset schema for profit margin

Following this step you should upload a file containing your product SKUs and their profit margins. Once this step is completed, you can create Custom Reports, as described in the previous example.

## Importing Refund Data

Refunds happen. To get your metrics as accurate as possible, you should upload the refunds into the system if and when they do happen. The Enhanced Ecommerce feature of Universal Analytics allows you to import Refund Data. The process is the same as before, but there is a specific dataset type for refunds in Google Analytics. In the case of refunds, the system limits the choices to a predefined set of commerce dimensions and metrics rather than your own custom ones.

Once you choose Refund Data from the dataset types options, you can select one or more data elements as part of your upload, choosing from Product SKU, Product Price, Quantity Refunded, and Revenue (as shown in Figure 7-9).

**Figure 7-9:** Uploading refund data into Google Analytics

Download the schema and upload the data as described in the previous content data example.

## Limitations and Best Practices

There are numerous advantages to using Data Import to improve the completeness and accuracy of your data. However, there are some things to keep in mind as you architect your solution:

- You may upload 50 total datasets per property.
- Data is limited to 50 uploads per day per property and 1GB max upload file size.

■ Data will be joined only for new hits as they are processed, except for refund and cost data that's treated as special cases. Google Analytics Premium users who select Query Time Processing have an additional option (see the sidebar at the end of this section).

■ Deleting a dataset means that future data won't be joined, *not* that previously joined data will be stripped from reports.

■ Filters will affect your imported data, so consider if and how they will affect your data. Also note that keys (such as URL) will be joined before any filter is applied.

■ Consider utilizing both Custom Dimensions and Custom Metrics.

■ You must have edit permissions to a Google Analytics property in order to upload data to it.

■ If you import an empty string, it will be interpreted as "not set" in the reports.

■ Real-time reports are not yet supported.

■ Not every dimension or metric is available. Specifically, custom variables, time-based dimensions (hour/minute/second), and geo-dimensions (country, city) are not available for widening.

■ No personally identifiable information (PII) may be uploaded under any circumstances.

■ Uploaded data needs to be processed before it can show up in reports. Once processing is complete, it may take up to 24 hours before the imported data will begin to be applied to incoming hit data.

---

**QUERY TIME VERSUS PROCESSING TIME**

Normally when a dataset is uploaded for import, the next time Google sees a hit that matches the key, that data is joined for that particular hit. Google Analytics Premium users have another desirable option called Query Time Processing, which immediately joins the matching data when a report requests that data. This means that historical data contained in the report is also joined, not just the new hits going forward. Also, data joined using Query Time will be reversed if the dataset is deleted.

At this time, Query Time Processing is only available to the campaign data, content data, and product data hit types and cannot be used with the following:

■ Remarketing audience exports
■ Datasets with date-based keys (for dimensions that change over time)
■ Unified segments
■ Multi-channel funnels
■ Cohort reporting
■ Real-time reports

## Summary

In this chapter you learned about the different ways to import data into Google Analytics and how they can be used. However, most of the chapter focused on Data Import, as it has four important advantages over other methods:

- There is no code to write, maintain, or publish.
- Data may not be available before the pageview hit is sent.
- Data may be confidential.
- It can accommodate larger sizes.

Following a description of all types of data that can be imported through the Data Import feature, you learned about a few real-world use cases where you might want to implement them. The following examples were described in-depth:

1. Importing content data
2. Importing product profit margin data
3. Importing refund data

Finally, you learned about some of the best practices and limitations when using Data Import to improve the completeness and accuracy of your data.

# 8

# User Data Integration

*This chapter was contributed by Kristoffer Olofsson, Partner at Precis Digital, an online intelligence and marketing agency. Kristoffer has a background as an implementation specialist in the Google Analytics Premium team. He has been working with data since his early university years and often serves as a link between digital managers and developers by speaking the language of both.*

Universal Analytics, the latest version of Google Analytics, enables a range of new capabilities that were difficult (if not impossible) to achieve in the past. Perhaps most excitingly, Universal Analytics provides you with the collection methodology necessary to measure journeys across multiple devices, and stitches it all together for you in an intuitive reporting interface that would require many development hours to produce.

In this chapter, you learn the concepts of leveraging Universal Analytics to this end: how to connect behavior data across devices using a common key, the User ID, and how you can piggyback on that connection to surface relevant business data from virtually any dataset alongside your online data.

## The Siloed Dataset

Businesses can have any number of datasets containing different types of information that are being evaluated on an ongoing basis. This could be financial data, Customer Relationship Management (CRM) system data, or any type of organized statistics and facts that are saved and stored over a given period of time. If such datasets are unique in terms of what dimensions or fields they contain, they inevitably exist in silos. This means they cannot be brought together to present one consolidated view.

In order to merge data, datasets must share a common *key* that joins them. The most prevalent of such keys is also part of the fundamental structure of the universe: *time*. Businesses constantly use it to join datasets: when looking at quarterly revenue by number of customers, when calculating which holiday leads to higher ticket sales, when comparing costs to earnings, and so on. The trick to putting such metrics side by side is that datasets share time dimensions, like dates, which enables side-by-side comparison.

However, a limitation of time as a dimension is that it is not granular enough to show how datasets fit together on an individual level; that is, for the users or customers who generated the data in the first place. For example, if you want to dig down into which users moved from one platform to another, a date dimension will be limited if your data is an aggregation of many different users without something to distinguish them as individuals. In this case, your statistical analyses will be limited to finding correlations and relationships between platform behaviors as a whole.

When dealing with Google Analytics data, a typical example of this challenge is when users move across different platforms and browsers. Their paths are nonlinear and unpredictable, and you cannot make sense of their full journeys. As a result, you probably miss important insights about your audiences. Without a key that combines the data from each platform and browser for each user, interactions across these will be siloed, and you will be unable to connect the dots in a meaningful way. You need something more than time—a more granular key. In a CRM database, this key is often a unique customer ID, which allows businesses to monitor customer behavior over time.

To leverage such an ID, it needs to be consistently present in all the datasets you want to combine. Unfortunately, the challenge doesn't stop here. Even if you have an ID stored somewhere for each of your customers as they identify themselves, you might not have the capacity to make sense of the data. Your users may log in online, purchase items in offline stores, or sign up for notifications in your app. But what if you don't have the necessary tools to stitch it all together, despite setting the same ID across all instances? This is where Google Analytics, as a data collection and reporting tool, is in a perfect position to address your problem.

## The User ID

Before learning more about cross-device tracking, it is important you understand the technicalities of how the Google Analytics tracking works. For each interaction tracked on Google Analytics, be it an event, a pageview, or a social interaction, an HTTP request (also known as a "hit") is sent to the Google Analytics servers. Each request becomes a row in a table stored on the servers, and then is tied together in sessions through a field called the Client ID. A hit is sent along with all the parameters necessary to create meaningful reports in Google Analytics. Among other things, this is what enables you to see how users move across your website or application in coherent sessions.

However, the Client ID is precisely that, a *client* identifier. A client in this case refers to a browser or a specific application. Your users may have several Client IDs, one for each client they use to access your platform or website. To be able to stitch sessions together *across* clients, you need a common key that all HTTP requests share, independent of the client. Enter the golden key: the User ID. A User ID does not identify the client; that job is already taken care of by the Client ID. The User ID identifies the individual using the client. See the relationship between the User and Client IDs in Figure 8-1.

A common misconception is that you can somehow use Google Analytics to surface cross-device user behavior without setting a common key like the User ID. This is not true; Google Analytics will always require you to set User IDs and pass them through to the servers in HTTP requests to be able to stitch data together across platforms. The only way to get consistent IDs in this manner is when your users identify themselves in one way or another (through a login, a purchase, or anything that says "this is me").

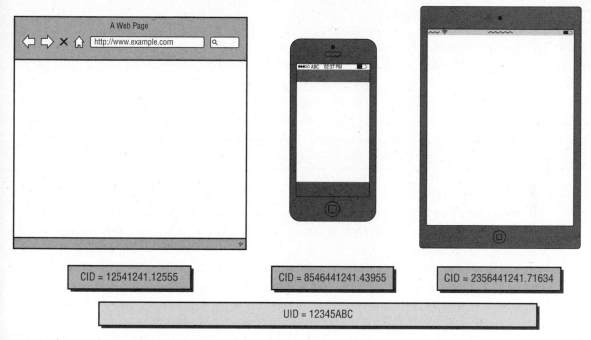

**Figure 8-1:** The relationship between Client and User IDs.

**WARNING** Please note that according to the Google Analytics Terms of Service, it is forbidden to send personally identifiable information to your Google Analytics account. You may use a unique identifier, but not a name, phone number, email address, social security number, or any other personally identifiable information. To learn more about it, read the full Terms of Service at http://goo.gl/t03xWG.

In the following sections you learn the steps required to start gathering and reporting user-level data with the User ID feature. The steps are:

1. **Create a User ID View**: This step shows how to create a User ID View and the extra reports you will get access to by using this feature.
2. **Set the User ID**: This step shows how to set the User ID when sending hits to Google Analytics.
3. **Store the User ID**: This step shows how to store the User ID in order to populate it as the value of a variable used by Google Analytics during collection.

Following those steps, you will learn how to import additional information into Google Analytics, such as CRM data, using the Measurement Protocol (which was briefly discussed in Chapter 7, "Custom Data Integration").

# Creating a User ID View

A User ID View reports data exclusively from sessions in which you send hits to Google Analytics including a User ID. This means that any session coming from an anonymous user would not be shown in the User ID View; however, your standard reports will still show your total number of users.

In order to create the User ID View, log in to your Google Analytics account and click on Admin at the top of your screen. Choose the Property you would like to use to collect the User ID sessions, and then click on the Tracking Info menu below the Property selector drop-down; choose User-ID. The process of creating a User ID View is composed of three different screens:

1. In the first screen you will be asked to review and agree to the User ID policy.
2. In the second screen you will be given explanations on how to implement the User ID, which we discuss below. You will also have the choice to change the *Session Unification* settings, which allow hits collected before the User ID is assigned to be associated with ID, so long as the hits are from the session in which an ID value is assigned for the first time. When set to OFF, only data with User IDs explicitly assigned can be associated. Learn more about session unification at `http://goo.gl/pWq1kX`.
3. In the third screen you will see a quick summary of what exactly a User ID View is.

After creating a User ID View, you will have access to four additional reports—three in the User ID View and one in the standard View: Device Overlap, Device Paths, and Acquisition Device in the User ID View, and User ID Coverage in the standard View. The following sections describe what each report will show you.

## The Device Overlap Report

This report, and the following two reports, can be found on the User ID View under the left-side menu named Audience, under a section named Cross Device.

This report shows a squared Venn diagram visualizing how users interact with the website, where the area of the rectangles represents the Users in each combination. There are several combinations, such as only through a mobile device, only through a tablet device, only through a desktop computer, and all possible variations.

You also have the option to view the same diagram with the area representing the revenue contributed to your business by the different device variations. This can provide insights into how each device (or group of devices) is performing. Apart from the diagram, as shown in Figure 8-2, you will also see a table below the visualization summarizing the data.

## The Device Paths Report

This report, shown in Figure 8-3, provides insight into the order users visited your website or app and how they performed based on their path. You can use both site usage- and conversion-related metrics to analyze each of the paths.

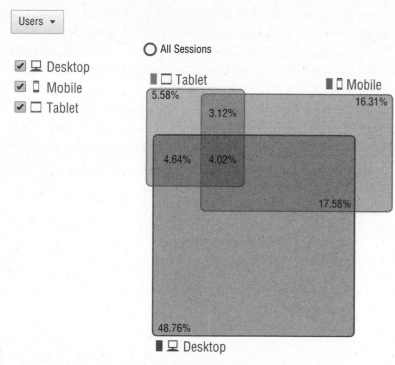

Users ▾

○ All Sessions

☑ 🖥 Desktop
☑ 📱 Mobile
☑ ▢ Tablet

▮ ▢ Tablet
5.58%

3.12%

▮ ▢ Mobile
16.31%

4.64%  4.02%

17.58%

48.76%

▮ 🖥 Desktop

**Figure 8-2:** Device Overlap report on User ID View.

| Steps in path ? | Unique Visitors ? ↓ | Visits ? | Average Duration of Visits per Visitor ? |
|---|---|---|---|
| | **1,987**<br>% of Total: 100.00% (1,987) | **3,148**<br>% of Total: 100.00% (3,148) | **00:04:59**<br>Site Avg: 00:04:59 (0.00%) |
| 1. Desktop | **1,707** (85.91%) | **2,548** (80.94%) | 00:05:04 |
| 2. Tablet | **113** (5.69%) | **137** (4.35%) | 00:04:39 |
| 3. Mobile | **103** (5.18%) | **127** (4.03%) | 00:05:19 |
| 4. Desktop Mobile | **15** (0.75%) | **56** (1.78%) | 00:04:42 |
| 5. Mobile Desktop | **9** (0.45%) | **21** (0.67%) | 00:03:55 |
| 6. Desktop Mobile Desktop | **7** (0.35%) | **34** (1.08%) | 00:03:34 |
| 7. Desktop Tablet | **6** (0.30%) | **18** (0.57%) | 00:09:59 |
| 8. Desktop Mobile Desktop Mobile | **3** (0.15%) | **20** (0.64%) | 00:04:02 |

☼ Path Options

**Figure 8-3:** Device Paths report on User ID View.

Using the Device Paths report, you might find out that specific devices are successful in different parts of the buying cycle. This can help you drive your ad strategy by advertising upper-funnel keywords on tablets and branded keywords on desktops, or vice versa if it makes sense based on your data. For some businesses, users might use mobile for research and desktop for purchasing, and for other businesses it might be the opposite.

An interesting capability provided in the Device Paths report is changing the path definitions. As you can see in Figure 8-4, you can adjust path options and the minimum steps to show in a path. You can either see the whole path or adjust the path to show only steps before and after the following:

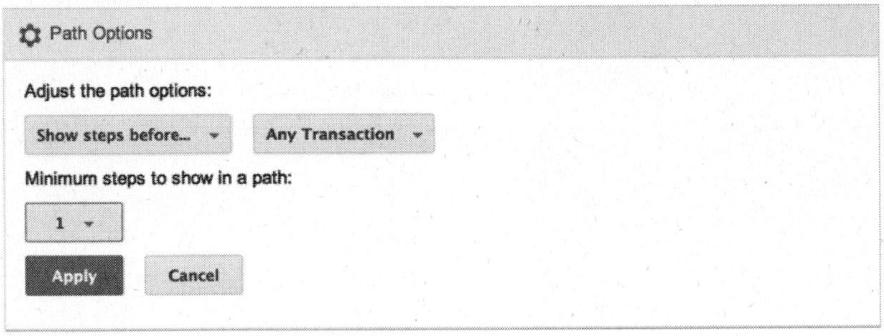

**Figure 8-4:** Paths options for Device Paths report.

- Any Goal Completion
- Any Transaction
- Event Action
- Event Category
- Event Label
- Page
- Goal

There are several use cases for each of them, but looking at all the devices used before a transaction would be especially interesting, as it would provide insights on how to optimize your device advertisement and functionality based on where in the funnel your most valuable users are.

## The Acquisition Device Report

This report, shown in Figure 8-5, provides insight into which devices are being successful in acquiring new users. The metrics show the revenue generated from the originating device, as opposed to revenue generated to subsequent devices used in the purchase cycle.

| Originating Device | Unique Visitors | Visits |
|---|---|---|
| | **1,842**<br>% of Total: 100.00% (1,842) | **2,869**<br>% of Total: 100.00% (2,869) |
| 1. Desktop | **1,616** (87.73%) | **2,529** (88.15%) |
| 2. Mobile | **116** (6.30%) | **188** (6.55%) |
| 3. Tablet | **110** (5.97%) | **152** (5.30%) |

**Figure 8-5:** Acquisition Device report on User ID View.

## The User-ID Coverage Report

Once you create the User ID View and start collecting data from User ID sessions, you will also have access to a new report on your standard Views, where you can monitor site usage and conversions for sessions including and excluding a User ID, as shown in Figure 8-6. You can find this report under the left-side menu named Audience, under a section named Behavior.

**Figure 8-6:** User ID Coverage Report on standard views.

# Setting the User ID

For Google Analytics to be able to stitch sessions together for any given individual user, each HTTP request must contain the User ID parameter uid. In the following code, you can see what a typical HTTP request to the Google Analytics servers looks like. Note that these requests follow the same structure on all platforms where a collection library built on top of the Measurement Protocol is implemented, including Universal Analytics. Learn more about it at http://goo.gl/leiE2q.

```
http://www.google-analytics.com/collect?
v=1&
tid=UA-12345-1&
cid=12345.6789&
t=pageview&
dl=exampleLocation&
uid=1234ABC
```

In this request, you can see the following parameters:

- Protocol version: `v`
- Tracking ID: `tid`
- Client ID: `cid`
- Hit type: `t`
- Document location: `dl` (this parameter can be replaced with document hostname, `dh`, plus document path, `dp`)
- User ID: `uid`

This type of request is generated automatically if you use one of the tracking libraries, such as `analytics.js` for websites or the `GoogleAnalyticsServices-library` for Android or iOS, and it sets a value for the `userId` field through the `uid` parameter. Here is an example using `analytics.js`; you would need to add the bold line of code:

```
ga('create', 'UA-12345-1');
ga(<set>, <userId>, <1234ABC>);
ga('send', 'pageview');
```

If you are using Google Tag Manager, you could first define the User ID value in the `dataLayer` above the GTM script, as follows:

```
<script>
    dataLayer = [{
        'userId': '1234ABC'
    }];
</script>
```

Then you set this as a field value in your tag, as shown in Figure 8-7.

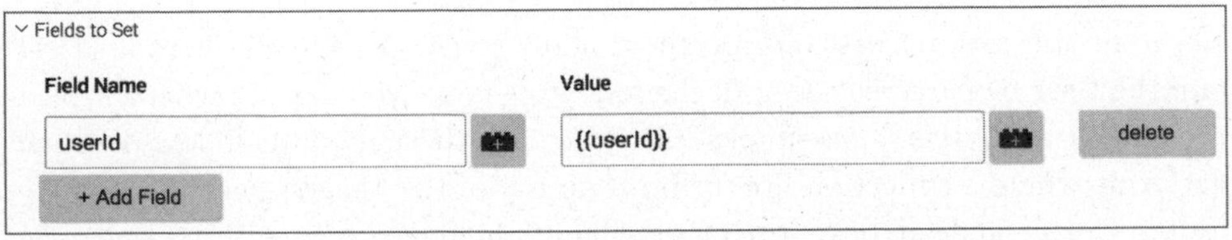

**Figure 8-7:** User ID tag on Google Tag Manager.

The Measurement Protocol is flexible enough to allow you to build requests on virtually any platform that can connect to the Internet. You just need to structure the requests in the same way as the tracking libraries, and data will be collected and reported.

## Storing the User ID

Since the unique ID for each user should be independent of the client being used, it cannot be stored, for example, as a cookie in the browser (which is the case with the Client ID value when using `analytics.js` for tracking websites).

For a business that already has unique IDs for each customer stored server-side, the most straightforward way is to populate this ID as the value of a variable subsequently used by Universal Analytics during collection. Naturally, you need to take the appropriate actions to ensure this value is assigned before a tracking method executes. Figure 8-8 shows the order in which the ID should be assigned to a user.

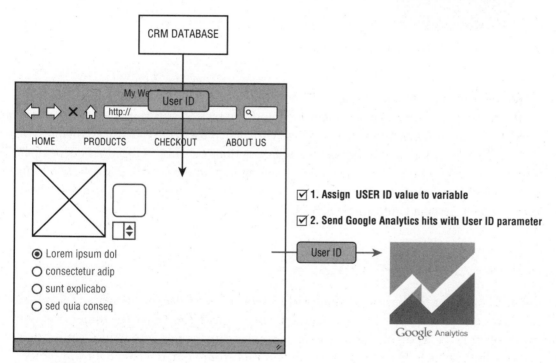

**Figure 8-8:** Storing the User ID to a website user.

For apps, you can leverage local data storage (such as the `SharedPreferences` class in Android) to store the same value when the user identifies herself. For all subsequent requests to the Google Analytics servers, the same value should be included in the User ID parameter (`&uid=`). Figure 8-9 shows a schematic description of how it would work on a mobile application.

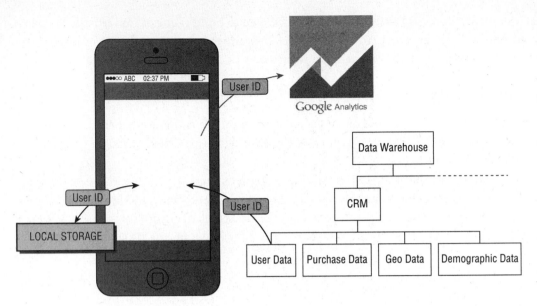

**Figure 8-9:** Storing the User ID to a mobile application user.

Note that *all* requests must include the User ID parameter for the request data to be included in reporting. It is not enough to set it once and hope for automatic session stitching; the ID will not be associated with subsequent requests if you leave it out. Only when users have identified themselves, for example through a login, should their sessions and interactions be stitched together independent of platform. As previously discussed in the section showing how to create a User ID View, all hits during the same session prior to when the user logged in will have the User ID associated with them, provided that you have Session Unification enabled.

## Importing Additional Data

Once you have figured out the best ways to identify users across platforms, you are in a golden position to import all types of data in your requests. Since you already have the dimension that will join it all together in reporting, and as long as you set this value consistently across platforms, you can simply attach additional values to requests from your internal data warehouse, website, apps, or virtually any system that can connect to the Internet. The Measurement Protocol is very flexible.

A good example of this is to leverage Custom Dimensions to populate business-specific data to your requests. Imagine you have a table in your CRM that looks like the one shown in Figure 8-10.

| Customer ID | Region | Member Status | Member Since | Purchases |
|---|---|---|---|---|
| g37iohg39h3 | NY | Bronze | 04/06/2013 | 4 |
| go43hg34oig | WA | Bronze | 01/05/2012 | 3 |
| ft3487f3873 | MI | Silver | 04/03/2009 | 8 |
| 3gulyufil43h | WA | Gold | 05/01/2014 | 10 |

**Figure 8-10:** Sample table from a CRM.

As you send requests using the Measurement Protocol, for example after an offline purchase by a member, you should include all relevant data in your requests. As long as the hit also includes the User ID (or in its absence, at least the Client ID), it will stitch together nicely with all the other data within Google Analytics for that user or client:

```
http://www.google-analytics.com/collect?
v=1&
tid=UA-12345-1&
cid=12345.6789&
t=pageview&
dl=exampleLocation&
uid=g37iohg39h3&
cd1=NY
cd2=Bronze
cd3=04/06/2013
cd4=4
```

In order to have this shown in your Google Analytics reports, you also need to change the Custom Dimension settings in your Admin interface. In order to do that, log in to your Google Analytics account and click on Admin at the top of your screen. Then, under Property, choose Custom Definitions and then Custom Dimensions. You will find a table similar to Figure 8-11. Click on + New Custom Dimension and choose User for the scope.

| + NEW CUSTOM DIMENSION | | 🔍 Search | | |
|---|---|---|---|---|
| **Custom Dimension Name** | **Index** ↓ | **Scope** | **Last Changed** | **State** |
| Newsletter | 1 | User | May 12, 2014 | Active |
| Reader | 2 | User | May 12, 2014 | Active |

**Figure 8-11:** Custom dimensions table on the Google Analytics Admin section.

Once you create the Custom Dimension, you will notice that it was assigned an index number (see the second column in Figure 8-11). The index of each Custom Dimension you create should be used in the code shown previously, where cd1 indicates index 1, cd2 indicates index 2, and so on.

Once you send the Custom Dimensions through the Measurement Protocol and enable them in the interface, you will have access to a more comprehensive picture of your customers, and your reports can be tailored to fit your business requirements. Figure 8-12 shows a sample table that you would now be able to build.

| Member Region (?) | Member Status (?) | Device Category (?) | Users ↓ |
|---|---|---|---|
| 1. NY | Bronze | desktop | **543** (0.17%) |
| 2. WA | Bronze | desktop | **350** (0.11%) |
| 3. SF | Silver | mobile | **342** (0.11%) |
| 4. NY | Bronze | mobile | **241** (0.08%) |

**Figure 8-12:** Tailored report on Google Analytics interface.

If the User ID is in place, you can combine your custom data with cross-device reporting as well. Figure 8-13 shows a sample report from Google Analytics in which information from a CRM was passed to Google Analytics through a Custom Dimension (Silver members) in order to show how those users move between device categories.

| Steps in path (?) | Users (?) ↓ | Revenue (?) | Transactions (?) | Revenue per User (?) |
|---|---|---|---|---|
| **Silver Members** | **104,037** <br> % of Total: 24.96% <br> (416,861) | **SEK3,445,007.42** <br> % of Total: 124.37% <br> (SEK2,770,013.69) | **33,115** <br> % of Total: <br> 99.60% (33,247) | **SEK8.09** <br> % of Total: 121.79% <br> (SEK6.64) |
| 1. Desktop | **207,588** (48.76%) | SEK1,020,675.70 (29.63%) | 15,376 (46.43%) | SEK4.92 (60.76%) |
| 2. Mobile | **69,431** (16.31%) | SEK619,392.95 (17.98%) | 3,927 (11.86%) | SEK8.92 (110.24%) |
| 3. Tablet | **23,749** (5.58%) | SEK60,946.37 (1.77%) | 408 (1.23%) | SEK2.57 (31.71%) |
| 4. Desktop Mobile | **15,190** (3.57%) | SEK80,471.44 (2.34%) | 1,408 (4.25%) | SEK5.30 (65.46%) |
| 5. Desktop Mobile Desktop | **11,856** (2.79%) | SEK100,552.25 (2.92%) | 1,445 (4.36%) | SEK8.48 (104.80%) |

**Figure 8-13:** Cross-device path based on CRM data.

An alternative to including additional Custom Dimensions in the actual requests is to leverage Data Import (discussed in the previous chapter), using the user ID as the key to import additional metadata about your customers. A benefit of this approach is that your requests will be smaller. However, you would need to perform the upload regularly to continuously include new customers as time goes by.

# Summary

In this chapter you learned about the process used to integrate different datasets into Google Analytics. The most important business case for such integration is the power to understand how your users behave across multiple devices and platforms. In order to create a robust cross-device measurement, you learned how to perform the following steps:

1. Create a User ID View.
2. Set the User ID.
3. Store the User ID.

Following those steps, you also learned how to import additional information into Google Analytics, such as CRM data, using the Measurement Protocol. This empowers you to report user behavior and website performance across devices, which can also include virtually any data you choose to send.

The following additional reports are available to you after you've completed the integration discussed in this chapter:

- The User ID View reports (Device Overlap, Device Paths, and Acquisition Device) show how users move between platforms where you have a presence and provide a holistic view of true audience behavior.
- User ID Coverage in the standard View provides an overall picture of what percentage of your users were assigned a User ID and the difference in behavior between "Assigned" and "Unassigned."
- Custom reporting enables you to bring in additional information from any dataset, as long as you can connect to the Internet and send data through requests to the Google Analytics servers.

# 9

# Marketing Campaign Data Integration

*This article was contributed by Benjamin Mangold, Director of Digital & Analytics at Loves Data, a digital analytics and online marketing agency based in Australia. He lives and breathes Google Analytics. He is a regular speaker on Google Analytics and Google AdWords topics and consults with leading brands on integrated online campaigns.*

In this chapter you learn how to integrate data from all your marketing campaigns into Google Analytics using both UTM parameters (discussed in Chapter 1, "Implementation Best Practices") and the Data Import feature.

The chapter starts with an overview of Google Analytics acquisition channels, and then provides best practices when it comes to tagging both online and offline marketing campaigns. Finally, you learn how to use the Data Import feature to upload all your marketing campaigns data into Google Analytics.

## Google Analytics Acquisition Channels

Google Analytics automatically measures a whole range of different ways people find your website. If you navigate to the Acquisition reports, you'll find insights about how people are finding you online. As shown in Figure 9-1, the Overview report provides a summary of these insights.

The default channel groupings you'll find in this report include:

- **Direct** most commonly includes people who know the URL of your website (and they open a new browser and type the URL). More generally, a session is attributed to direct traffic when no information about the referral source is available or when the referring source or search term has been configured to be ignored (see the "Excluding Referrals" section in Chapter 1.)
- **Organic Search** shows you the people who have clicked through from an organic listing on a search engine.
- **Referral** groups people who find your website by clicking on a link on another website. (For example, if someone links to your website in a blog post or a comment in a forum.)
- **Social** indicates people who navigate to your website using a link from a social network.

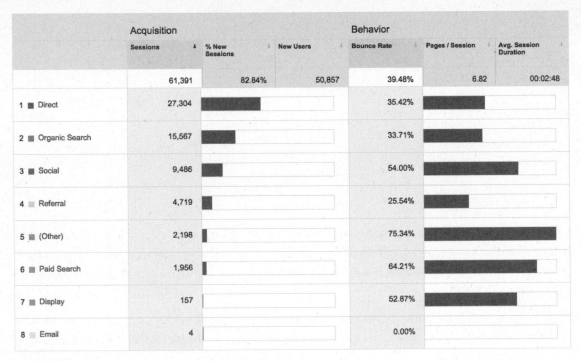

| | Acquisition | | | Behavior | | |
|---|---|---|---|---|---|---|
| | Sessions ↓ | % New Sessions ↓ | New Users ↓ | Bounce Rate ↓ | Pages / Session ↓ | Avg. Session Duration ↓ |
| | 61,391 | 82.84% | 50,857 | 39.48% | 6.82 | 00:02:48 |
| 1 ■ Direct | 27,304 | | | 35.42% | | |
| 2 ■ Organic Search | 15,567 | | | 33.71% | | |
| 3 ■ Social | 9,486 | | | 54.00% | | |
| 4 ■ Referral | 4,719 | | | 25.54% | | |
| 5 ■ (Other) | 2,198 | | | 75.34% | | |
| 6 ■ Paid Search | 1,956 | | | 64.21% | | |
| 7 ■ Display | 157 | | | 52.87% | | |
| 8 ■ Email | 4 | | | 0.00% | | |

**Figure 9-1:** Google Analytics Acquisition reports overview

**NOTE** To learn how campaign and traffic source data is processed and populated in Google Analytics reports, visit `http://goo.gl/CmkZJN`.

Once you've linked your Google AdWords account to Google Analytics, as explained in Chapter 2, "AdWords Integration," you will be able to see these additional channel groupings:

- **Paid Search** indicates your linked Google AdWords account or other tracked paid ads.
- **Display** is similar to Paid Search, but for text, image, and rich media ads placed on the Google Display Network or other ad networks.

You can also customize your channel grouping to compare the performance of your branded and generic paid keywords, as explained in Chapter 2. Your company and product names are "brand" terms, while descriptive words are considered "generic." For example, Google is a branded keyword, while search engine is a generic keyword.

To do this, navigate to Admin and select Manage Brand Terms in the Channel Settings option in the right column. You can then add custom brand terms and terms that are automatically suggested by Google Analytics. Once you have defined your brand terms you will see the Branded Paid Search and Generic Paid Search channels displayed in your report.

The Acquisition reports (shown in Figure 9-1) can also include additional custom campaign data. Chapter 1 briefly discussed best practices when it comes to tagging custom campaigns with UTM parameters. This is important to implement before integrating your custom marketing campaign data. More detailed campaign tagging is discussed in the next section, but if you see the following rows, chances are you already use campaign tags.

- **Email** is for any inbound marketing campaign that Google Analytics sees as coming from email. For example, if you have a campaign-tagged URL in your email newsletter that includes email.
- **(Other)** is for any campaign-tagged URLs that fall outside of the other channel groupings.

**NOTE** You can customize channel groupings based on your own specific requirements. For example, if you want to see a channel grouping specifically for ads you are running on Twitter, you can create a custom group only for Twitter. To create a custom group, navigate to Admin and select Channel Grouping from the Channel Settings option. It is best to leave the default grouping and instead select + New Channel Grouping. This will prevent the default groupings from being modified accidentally.

## Tagging Custom Marketing Campaigns

Campaign tags allow you to measure your own custom marketing initiatives with Google Analytics, enabling you to extend beyond the standard traffic sources and marketing channels found in standard reports. Custom campaign tags can be used for any inbound marketing campaign you are running and are commonly used for measuring the following:

- Email campaigns
- Social media ads
- Non-AdWords CPC (cost-per-click)
- Offline campaigns

In order to measure these campaigns, you need to modify the inbound links that direct people to your website or app. By adding additional details to the end of these links, Google Analytics can report on the campaigns that they are a part of. These additional details (query parameters) are called UTM campaign tags.

Let's say you are running an ad on LinkedIn that directs people to your website. Your existing ad might have a destination URL such as the following:

```
http://www.mysite.com/contact-us
```

But you can modify this URL to include campaign tags, ending up with a URL such as:

```
http://www.mysite.com/contact-us?utm_source=linkedin.com&utm_medium=social&utm_
campaign=linkedin%20ads
```

This would allow you to see the following details inside Google Analytics reports:

| Source | Medium | Campaign |
| --- | --- | --- |
| linkedin.com | social | linkedin ads |

Campaign tags allow you to define a source, medium, and campaign name, along with optional keyword and content parameters. Since you define all of these elements, you have control over what will be displayed in your reports as people click through to your website. You can read about details of each custom tag parameter in the "Tagging Custom Campaigns" section in Chapter 1.

**WARNING**    Campaign tags should be used only for inbound marketing, and not in your own website. This is because when people click on a campaign-tagged link, a new session is reported inside Google Analytics. If you want to measure internal banners and promotions on your own website, you should use Event Tracking or Promotions with Enhanced Ecommerce. Learn more about Event Tracking at `http://goo.gl/ZkAqzv` and about Enhanced Ecommerce at `http://goo.gl/Gp5fZY`.

Remember that whatever you define for your campaign tag values will be displayed on your reports. It can be a good idea to open the Acquisition section (left sidebar on your Google Analytics interface) and navigate to the All Traffic and Campaigns report (see Figure 9-2), because this is where the values of your campaign tags appear. Use this link to access the report directly `http://goo.gl/Ni851C`.

Take the time to ask yourself what you want to see in these reports, since whatever you define as your source, medium, campaign, and optional term and content will be displayed there.

| | Campaign ? | Acquisition | |
| --- | --- | --- | --- |
| | | Sessions ? ↓ | % New Sessions ? |
| | | **3,973**<br>% of Total:<br>6.47% (61,391) | **91.39%**<br>Site Avg:<br>82.84%<br>(10.32%) |
| ☐ | 1.  Email Newsletter | **1,122** (28.24%) | 16.00% |
| ☐ | 2.  LinkedIn Ads | **999** (25.14%) | 94.69% |
| ☐ | 3.  Newspaper Ads | **873** (21.97%) | 92.90% |

**Figure 9-2:** Google Analytics campaign report

**NOTE** Using a consistent naming convention for your campaign-tagged links makes your reports easier to read. For example, the following campaign would appear as three different campaigns:

- `utm_campaign=LinkedInAds`
- `utm_campaign=linkedin-ads`
- `utm_campaign=linkedin_ads`

You should also consider adding a filter to convert all UTM values to lowercase to prevent duplicate entries for any instances where the same campaign values have been accidentally named using different casing. You can see how to add this filter in the "Eliminating Duplicate Pages" section in Chapter 1.

## Measuring Online Campaigns

Let's look at some different ways to use campaign tags for your online marketing campaigns. These are best practice guidelines that can be tweaked and modified to meet your own specific reporting requirements.

Measuring people who click through from your email newsletters and promotions is an important starting point. There is no single way to campaign-tag these links, but one option is to use the `source` to define the particular edition you are sending out to people. Try to keep the `medium` short and simple (this example uses `email`). You can then define your own campaign `name` and use the optional `content` parameter to distinguish individual links in your email. The optional `term` is left blank because this should only be used for search-based keywords from non-AdWords paid search marketing. See the example in the following table.

| Source | Medium | Campaign | Term | Content |
|--------|--------|----------|------|---------|
| july 2015 | `email` | email newsletter | | article link |
| july 2015 | `email` | email newsletter | | image |

Now you can use the Google Analytics URL Builder at `http://goo.gl/0iPxIA` to create your campaign-tagged links and then place them in your email newsletter.

**NOTE** Most email newsletter systems, like MailChimp and Campaign Monitor, allow you to automatically tag URLs with UTMs in your emails. Check out their support pages and ensure that you are happy with the way they automatically tag your links. If you want complete flexibility, manually tagging links is typically the best option.

Campaign-tagging your non-AdWords CPC campaigns allows you to compare the performance of the different networks. For example, if you're running search ads on Bing, you can also tag your destination URLs so you know these clicks are not reported as organic. You'll notice that the optional `term` and `content` parameters include some special elements—these automatically include the keyword you are bidding on and the ID of the particular ads clicked. You can then customize the campaign name to reflect your particular needs.

| Source | Medium | Campaign | Term | Content |
|--------|--------|----------|------|---------|
| bing.com | cpc | bing ads | {keyword} | ad {AdID} |

If you're running ads on social media, you should also tag the inbound links. Here are two examples:

| Source | Medium | Campaign | Term | Content |
|--------|--------|----------|------|---------|
| linkedin.com | social | linkedin ads | | ad description |
| facebook.com | social | facebook ads | | ad description |

Defining the medium as `social` allows you to see click-throughs from your ads in the campaigns reports, as well as in the dedicated social reports in the Acquisition section. Again, you will want to customize the campaign `name` and `content` parameters.

## Measuring Offline Campaigns

You can also measure offline campaigns that direct people to your website using campaign tags. Let's say you're placing an ad in the local newspaper for a special offer and you want people to visit your website. You can set up a special URL that redirects people to your landing page along with your campaign tags.

For example, your landing page might be located here:

```
http://www.mysite.com/offer/summer-promotion
```

And you create a campaign-tagged URL like so:

```
http://www.mysite.com/offer/summer-promotion?utm_source=newspaper&utm_
medium=offline&utm_campaign=newspaper%20ad
```

The next step is to work with your web developer to set up an URL redirect, avoiding the need to include a long, unsightly URL in your print ad. This means you can set up an URL such as:

```
http://www.mysite.com/promotion
```

The short URL would then redirect to your tagged URL.

Alternatively, you can consider using a URL shortener to create short links that redirect to any link you provide. Google offers such a service for free at `http://goo.gl` (used throughout this book), but if you want to use a customized short URL, you can also try `http://bit.ly`.

The following are a few examples of campaign tags for newspaper ads, brochures, and billboards:

| Source | Medium | Campaign | Term | Content |
|---|---|---|---|---|
| newspaper | offline | newspaper ad | | |
| brochure | offline | print brochure | | |
| billboard | offline | billboard ad | | |

The main thing to remember is to define your `source`, `medium`, and `campaign` clearly so that they are not confused with your online ads. In most cases, you will want to leave the optional `term` and `content` blank.

# Cost Data Import

Unlike Google AdWords reports, campaigns measured using campaign-tagged URLs do not include details about what happens before people click through to your website. For example, in Google AdWords reports you can see the number of impressions of your ads and the click-through rate (CTR). This is where Cost Data Import comes in, as it allows you to import data about your custom campaigns. Cost Data is one of the dataset types that can be integrated to Google Analytics through the Data Import feature (as described in Chapter 7, "Custom Data Integration").

Uploading details like impressions, CTR, and cost for your custom campaigns is important, especially if you are running Google AdWords campaigns—they give you additional context when evaluating the success of all your marketing initiatives. For example, if you are running paid campaigns through Google AdWords, Facebook, LinkedIn, and Twitter, you need to be able to compare the conversion rate against the cost of running the campaigns. This allows you to understand the ROI (return on investment) that different marketing initiatives are generating. You can use that information to make smart decisions about future budget allocations.

You always had the ability to export data from Google AdWords and Google Analytics in order to compare campaign performance. You can even export the data from your custom campaigns and merge the additional data inside Google Drive or Excel, but this can be a tedious process. This is where Google Analytics Cost Data Import comes in. You can use it to import the extra pieces of data that belong to your non-AdWords paid campaigns. This means you can quickly evaluate the performances of all your campaigns and compare advertising costs and ROI, right in the Google Analytics interface.

**NOTE** The reports created from your uploaded data don't provide the same granular detail available in the Google AdWords reports (like ad groups and individual keywords), but they do enable you to start performing top-level analysis within Google Analytics. Another point to remember is that the reports also rely on people actually traveling through to your website, so if you have impression data without any clicks, you won't get additional insights from the reports.

## The Cost Data Import Process

Before you start, it's important to understand that custom data is uploaded to a property inside Google Analytics and is then applied to one or more views, as shown in Figure 9-3. If you have a large-scale implementation, you will have to repeat the process if you want data available within views that are contained in different properties. For most cases, this won't be needed, but it is good to remember that upload is at the property level and not the account level.

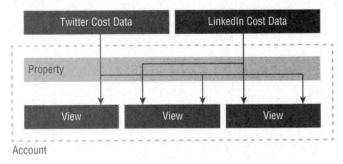

**Figure 9-3:** The Import Data scheme

Another critical thing to check is that you are using campaign tags on your inbound links to ensure that you can match your cost data to data that is available from your Google Analytics reports. The campaign tags you use will become the key that you use to combine the data inside your reports.

In the following sections, you learn how to import Cost Data into Google Analytics, *starting from the second step in the following list*, as the first step was already discussed in the previous section.

1. Ensure that you are using UTM campaign tags.
2. Download cost data from non-AdWords sources.
3. Set up your custom dataset.
4. Format your data for upload.
5. Upload your data into Google Analytics.

### Step 2: Download Cost Data from Non-AdWords Sources

Unless you already know what data is available for your custom campaigns, the best starting point is to download the data you have available before configuring the dataset inside Google Analytics. If you are running ads on third-party advertising networks, such as LinkedIn, Facebook, and Twitter, you should be able to download Clicks, Cost, and Impressions at a minimum.

**LinkedIn**    If you are going to upload data for your LinkedIn ads, you first need to download the data from LinkedIn Campaign Manager. You can find this under the Reporting tab, as shown in Figure 9-4.

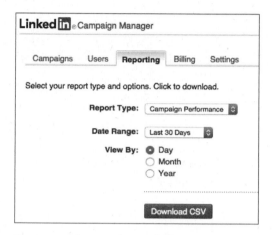

**Figure 9-4:** Downloading data from the LinkedIn Campaign Manager

**Facebook**    Within the Facebook Ads Manager, click on Reports in the menu on the left and ensure that the current report is set to General Metrics with campaign-level reporting, as shown in Figure 9-5. Next, click on Breakdown and select Daily. You can now select Export and select the CSV option.

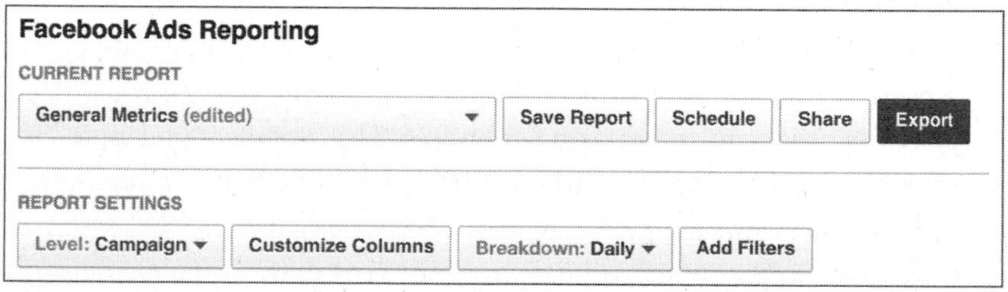

**Figure 9-5:** Downloading data from Facebook Ads reporting

**Twitter**    Log into your Twitter Ads account, select the appropriate date range, and then click Export. This will allow you to download a CSV that gives a daily breakdown for your campaigns (see Figure 9-6).

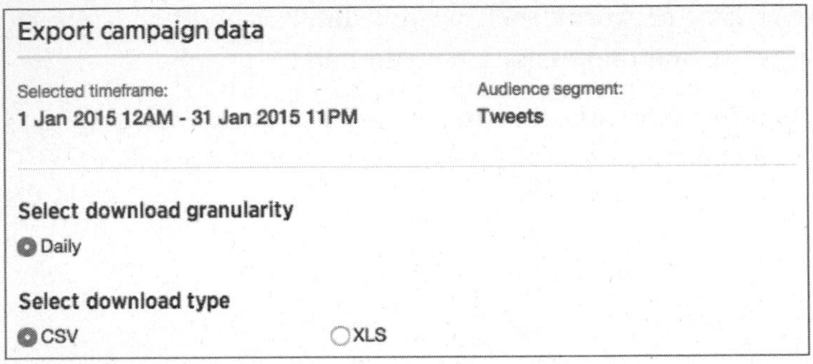

**Figure 9-6:** Downloading Twitter campaign data

**NOTE** Not using LinkedIn, Facebook, or Twitter? Try to download a CSV report from your advertising platform. If it's not available, you can use another format, but it might mean a little more work formatting the data.

## Step 3: Set Up Your Custom Dataset

The next step is to set up the custom dataset. To do this, start by navigating to the Admin section and selecting the appropriate property.

Within the property, select Data Import, click the + New Data Set button, select Cost Data, and then click Next Step. Now you will need to name the dataset and select the view(s) where you want this data to be available. Following this step, you will see a screen similar to Figure 9-7.

For example, if you are going to upload cost data from ads on LinkedIn, you would create a new dataset called LinkedIn, which would then store all of your LinkedIn data. In most cases, you'll need to create multiple custom datasets for each of your advertising channels. This means if you advertise on LinkedIn, Facebook, and Twitter, you need to create three separate datasets. You can read more about Data Import limitations and specifications at http://goo.gl/3k1hdm.

Now you should configure the dataset so that when you import your cost data, Google Analytics reads the correct data into your reports and assigns your cost data to the correct ads.

You need to select the columns of data that you have available from the data that you previously downloaded. At a minimum, you need Medium, Source, and either Impressions, Clicks, or Cost. In most cases, you will want to add all of these in order to gain more insight from the data.

If you open the report downloaded for the LinkedIn example, you can see you have columns for Impressions, Total Clicks, and Total Spend, which you can use for Impressions, Clicks, and Cost. Since this data is from LinkedIn, it is safe to assume that Medium is CPC, as you are paying for the clicks, and Source is linkedin.com, because that is where your ads have been displayed. For LinkedIn, you can also use Ad Content for each ad variation and Destination URL, which is the landing page where users land from the ads.

**Figure 9-7:** Setting up a custom dataset

If you select Medium, Source, Campaign, Ad Content, or Keyword for columns in your dataset, each of these needs to directly correspond to UTM campaign tags that are already available on your reports (before you upload data).

For example, if you don't set any UTM campaign tags for your LinkedIn campaigns, and then define values for these parameters within your CSV for upload, the data still won't correspond to anything on your reports.

The Import Behavior option (see the bottom of Figure 9-7) you select tells Google Analytics what to do if you upload multiple pieces of data for the same day. For example, Summation sums the uploaded data; if you uploaded a dataset for $10 on January 1, 2015 and then later uploaded another dataset with a value of $15, these would be summed to equal $25.

When you are happy with the columns, click the Get Schema button. This will show you the first line that is needed in your CSV file. You can also click the Download Schema Template button to get this in Excel format.

Once you have the header for your CSV file, you need to get all of the data into that format. For example, if your schema header looks like this:

```
ga:date,ga:medium,ga:source,ga:adClicks,ga:adCost,ga:impressions
```

Then this means the first column needs to contain the date, the second column the medium, the third column the source, and so on. The schema tells you what you will need inside your CSV spreadsheet before you upload it to Google Analytics.

**NOTE** Each custom dataset you create will have a unique ID or key, which is used to ensure that uploaded data ends up in the right dataset. Data can be uploaded at any time and you can view historical uploads by selecting History.

## Step 4: Format Your Data for Upload

If you are working in a spreadsheet (before exporting to CSV format), you will have something along the following lines:

| ga:data | ga:medium | ga:source | ga:adClick | ga:adCost | ga:impressions |
|---------|-----------|-----------|------------|-----------|----------------|
|         |           |           |            |           |                |
|         |           |           |            |           |                |

You need to get the data you have into the correct format. You might need to adjust some values so that Google Analytics accepts them. This includes the first column, which needs to be the date. Each day should be a row on your spreadsheet and the date needs to be in the format of year, month, and day. Data for December 29, 2014 would be formatted as 20141229. For example:

| ga:data  | ga:medium | ga:source    | ga:adClick | ga:adCost | ga:impressions |
|----------|-----------|--------------|------------|-----------|----------------|
| 20141229 | cpc       | linkedin.com | 135        | 302.4     | 10732          |
| 20141230 | cpc       | linkedin.com | 93         | 90.21     | 3090           |

If you have been working in Excel or Google Drive, you need to export this as a CSV file ready for upload. This will give you a file that contains something like this:

```
ga:date,ga:medium,ga:source,ga:adClicks,ga:adCost,ga:impressions
20141229,cpc,linkedin.com,135,302.4,10732
20141230,cpc,linkedin.com,93,90.21,3090
```

You are now ready to upload the data into Google Analytics.

### Step 5: Upload Your Data into Google Analytics

Navigate back to Admin within Google Analytics and select Data Import. You will see the name of the dataset you previously created, as shown in Figure 9-8.

| + NEW DATA SET | | Q Search | |
|---|---|---|---|
| **Name** | **Type** | **Data Set ID** | **Action** |
| LinkedIn | Cost Data | EwLfwHL0RGiD3zrJ... | Manage uploads |

**Figure 9-8:** Uploading campaign data into Google Analytics

Select Manage Uploads and then click Upload File and Choose Files. This allows you to select and upload the CSV you created. Your cost data will now be uploaded and processed into your reports.

> **NOTE**  You can also upload your cost data using the Google Analytics Management API. For details, visit `http://goo.gl/13XTiS`.

## Analyzing Marketing Campaigns

From here you can begin analyzing the campaign performance within Google Analytics. The Cost Analysis report is available in the Acquisition section. This report automatically calculates CTR and average CPC from your click and impression data, as shown in Figure 9-9.

| | Source / Medium ? | Sessions ? ↓ | Impressions ? | Clicks ? | Cost ? | CTR ? |
|---|---|---|---|---|---|---|
| | | **43,962**<br>% of Total: 100.00% (43,962) | **10,170,872**<br>% of Total: 100.00% (10,170,872) | **5,731**<br>% of Total: 100.00% (5,731) | **$340,851.44**<br>% of Total: 100.00% ($340,851.44) | **0.18%**<br>Avg for View: 0.18% (0.00%) |
| ☐ | 1.  google / cpc | **15,979** (36.35%) | 1,106,209 (15.07%) | 98,002 (21.50%) | $109,384.06 (11.38%) | 8.86% |
| ☐ | 2.  twitter.com / social | **11,004** (25.03%) | 2,618,736 (36.14%) | 54,372 (14.34%) | $77,381.50 (8.97%) | 2.08% |
| ☐ | 3.  linkedin.com / social | **9,204** (20.94%) | 617,004 (8.37%) | 3,493 (0.59%) | $28,045.00 (3.10%) | 0.57% |

**Figure 9-9:** Cost Analysis report

It's important to ensure you have your goals configured (and ecommerce if you are selling online), as this will give you the data that you need in order to analyze marketing acquisition performance, including return-per-click (RPC), return on investment (ROI), and margin. When using these metrics, remember that they are calculated against your advertising cost, so they will not include any costs or investment other than the actual amount you paid for the clicks.

You might want to consider exporting this data into Google Drive and performing your own calculations, so you can factor in elements like human resources (the amount of time needed to create and manage your campaigns), profit margin (if you are focused on ecommerce transactions), and even customer lifetime value (CLV).

Whatever you decide, you want to identify campaigns that have a higher likelihood to convert, along with higher value (where you look at ROI and CLV). Once you identify your top-performing campaigns, you can begin to perform more in-depth analysis on the poor performing campaigns and start incrementally testing campaign changes to see if you can improve performance.

## Summary

In this chapter you learned how to integrate marketing campaign data into Google Analytics in order to understand how different campaigns compare not only in terms of traffic, but also in terms of overall results.

In order to integrate the data you need to perform two main steps:

1. **Tag your campaign links with UTM parameters:** This step enables you to start understanding traffic patterns from your campaigns and will later be used as the *key* to merge the cost data imported.
2. **Import cost data to Google Analytics:** This step consists of downloading data from your non-AdWords advertising campaigns and uploading this data into Google Analytics in order to enrich your acquisition reports.

Once you have completed these steps, you will be able to start analyzing and comparing CTR, average CPC, and other metrics across your entire advertising traffic.

# 10

# A/B Testing Data Integration

*This chapter was contributed by Peep Laja, an entrepreneur and conversion-optimization professional. He runs an optimization agency, and blogs at ConversionXL.com.*

There are many A/B testing tools available for website owners and marketers that make testing easy. These tools just run tests; they are not exactly designed for post-test analysis. Most testing tools have gotten better over the years, but they still lack many of the features provided by Google Analytics.

In this chapter, you learn how to integrate data from Optimizely, a widely used A/B testing tool, into Google Analytics. The tool is used as an example; if you use a different testing tool, check its support center to learn how to integrate it into Google Analytics.

## Integrating Optimizely Data into Google Analytics

Optimizely comes with a built-in Google Analytics integration, and data for each test should be sent to Google Analytics. This is not only to enhance your analysis capabilities, but also to help you be more confident about the veracity of your data. Your testing tool might be recording the data incorrectly, and if you have no other source for your test data, you can never be sure whether to trust it.

You set up the integration in Optimizely from the project settings, as shown in Figure 10-1.

**NOTE**    You definitely want to use Universal Analytics (`analytics.js`) instead of the previous version of Google Analytics (`ga.js`). If you haven't upgraded your Google Analytics yet, do so as soon as you can. Not only will you be able to take advantage of various Google Analytics features, you will also have up to 20 Custom Dimension slots for measuring concurrent A/B tests sending data to Google Analytics. With the previous version, you have only five. You can learn how to upgrade in the Universal Analytics Upgrade Center at `http://goo.gl/EBQ5BR`.

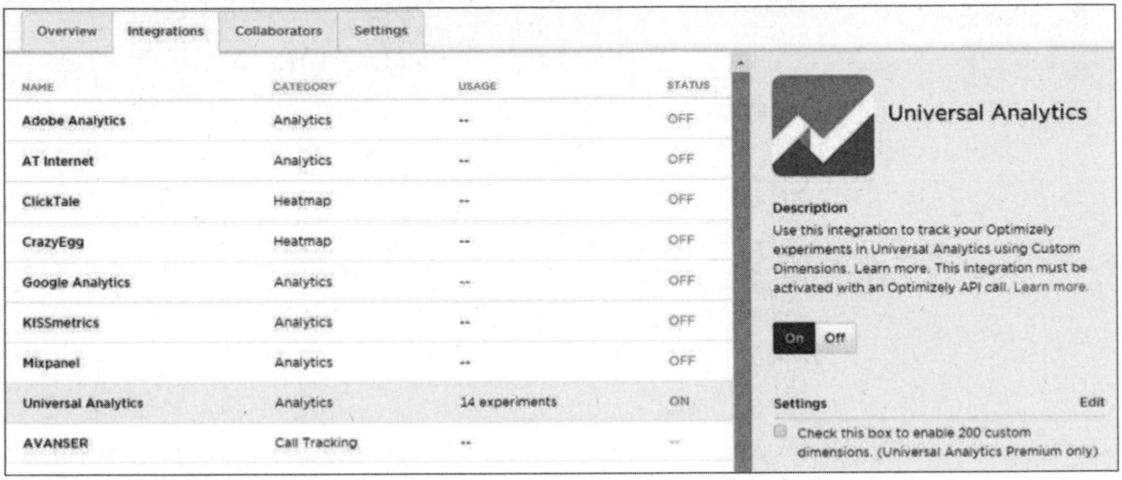

**Figure 10-1:** Setting up Universal Analytics integration in Optimizely

Note that once you finish this step, you need to visit your Admin interface on Google Analytics and create a Custom Dimension as well. To do so, log in to Google Analytics and click on Admin on the top of your screen. Then choose the property you are using to send data from the test; look for a menu named Custom Definitions and click on Custom Dimensions under it. Finally, create a new dimension and take note of the slot number. That's the number you will enter on the bottom-left drop-down shown in Figure 10-2.

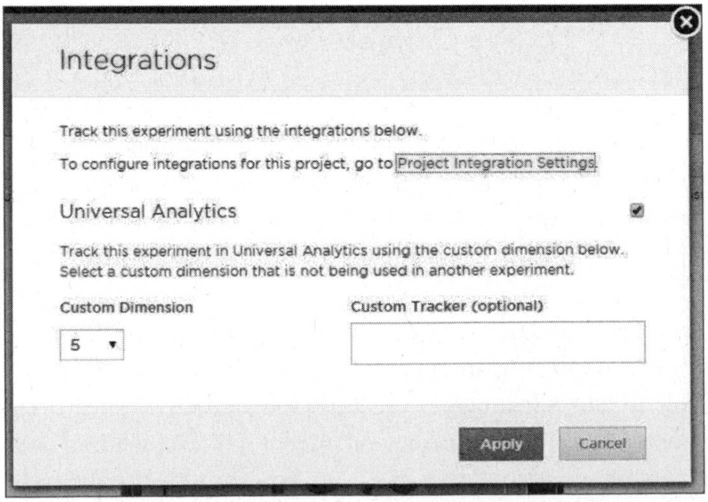

**Figure 10-2:** Choosing custom dimensions for each test

Make sure that there aren't multiple tests using the same Custom Dimension slot (or Custom Variable if you are using a previous version) in Google Analytics. They will overwrite each other's data, and you won't be able to trust that data anymore, so be sure to use only one test per slot at any given time.

**WARNING** When you choose a slot for a Custom Dimension, make sure that another team is not using the same slot. It is common to use Custom Dimensions to measure several user, session, and page attributes. If your business is currently not using Custom Dimensions, you should re-think your Google Analytics implementation. Learn more about the power of Custom Dimensions (and Metrics) in the detailed case study at `http://goo.gl/5hGZb9`.

You can find a step-by-step guide for this integration on the Optimizely support website, including how to set up Custom Dimensions. Check out `http://goo.gl/iJG57x`.

Once you finish performing these steps, you will be able to analyze any test result in Google Analytics using Custom Reports. You can make the report show you almost any analytics data you want. See the example in Figure 10-3.

| GA05 | Users | Revenue per User | Ecommerce Conversion Rate | Average QTY | Average Order Value | Transactions | Revenue |
|---|---|---|---|---|---|---|---|
| | 67,359<br>% of Total:<br>100.00%<br>(67,359) | $64.81<br>% of Total:<br>976.59% ($6.64) | 39.31%<br>Site Avg:<br>4.37%<br>(800.37%) | 2.23<br>Site Avg:<br>2.12<br>(5.57%) | $122.75<br>Site Avg:<br>$121.64<br>(0.91%) | 2,113<br>% of Total:<br>57.50% (3,675) | $259,378.55<br>% of Total: 58.02%<br>($447,033.57) |
| 1. Optimizely_Cart_Noise_reduction_GA05<br>(2215293204): Variation_1 | 1,357 (33.91%) | $66.39(102.43%) | 40.33% | 2.18 | $122.74 | 734 (34.74%) | $90,088.92 (34.73%) |
| 2. Optimizely_Cart_Noise_reduction_GA05<br>(2215293204): Variation_2 | 1,338 (33.43%) | $63.27 (97.63%) | 39.90% | 2.38 | $119.07 | 711 (33.65%) | $84,660.84 (32.64%) |
| 3. Optimizely_Cart_Noise_reduction_GA05<br>(2215293204): Original | 1,307 (32.66%) | $64.75 (99.90%) | 37.68% | 2.13 | $126.69 | 668 (31.61%) | $84,628.79 (32.63%) |

**Figure 10-3:** Custom report showing Optimizely analysis on Google Analytics

Does one variation have more revenue per user? Why is that? Well, let's look at average cart value or average quantity. Those metrics can shed some light here. Use whatever metrics are useful in your particular case. To learn more about what Custom Reports are and how to build them, visit `http://goo.gl/3JxnB8`.

## Sending Test Variations as Events for Advanced Segmentation

By default, the Optimizely integrations with Google Analytics add a session-level Custom Dimension containing the Experiment Name and Variation Name that the user is currently bucketed into. As discussed in the previous session, this can be used to track which variations are performing best by creating Custom Reports on Google Analytics.

However, the integrations discussed are not foolproof. Sometimes the data is not passed on, and there can be up to 50% discrepancy (worst-case scenario). Somewhere, somehow, part of the data was lost for numerous reasons.

One particularly interesting trick for double-checking your data is to send an event to Google Analytics each time a variation is loaded (the credit for this idea goes to my good friend Ton Wesseling). This ensures that the Google Analytics tracking code gets all the information once it loads.

All you need to do is to add one line of code to the test's Global JavaScript (executed for all variations), plus a line of Event Tracking code on the last line of each test variation. This is the line you should add to the Global Experiment JavaScript console:

```
window.ga=window.ga||function(){(window.ga.q=window.ga.q||[])
    .push(arguments);};window.ga.l=+new Date();
```

In order to add this code to Optimizely, first open the experiment settings while editing a test, as shown in Figure 10-4. Choose Experiment JavaScript and add the code in the text field.

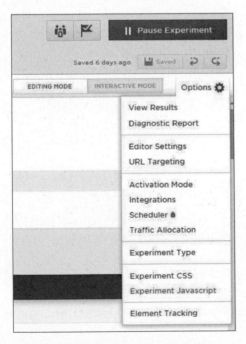

**Figure 10-4:** Adding JavaScript code to each experiment

You then need to add a line of Event Tracking code at the end of each variation (including the original). The following line shows a sample script, but note that you need to change the value of the experiment ID (where you see exp-2207684569) and the name of the variation (where you see Variation1):

```
window.ga('send', 'event', 'Optimizely', 'exp-2207684569',
  'Variation1', {'nonInteraction': 1});
```

The code will send an event to Google Analytics where the event category is Optimizely, the event action is the experiment ID (you can get that from your URL while editing a test), and the event label is Variation1 (can also be Original, Variation2, and so on.) Non-interaction means that no engagement is recorded on Google Analytics; otherwise, your bounce rate for experiment pages would be 0%.

Figure 10-5 shows how to add the code line to each variation in the Optimizely interface.

**Figure 10-5:** Adding events to each test variation

Now you can create segments in Google Analytics for each of the variations. Figure 10-6 shows a sample segment setup where you include only the behavior of users who viewed the original page in your test. Note that if you create such a segment, you need to change the event action to include your own experiment ID. You can learn more about how to create segments on Google Analytics at http://goo.gl/MburGD.

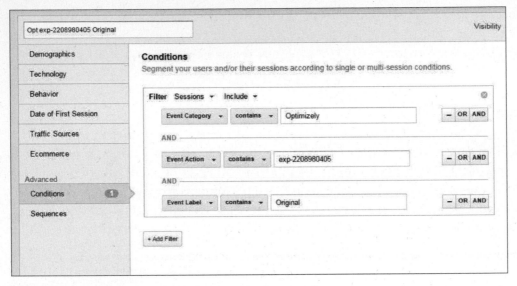

**Figure 10-6:** Segment including original alternative only

You should repeat the segment creation for each of your experiment versions and apply them onto any report. This will allow you to compare, side by side, the behavior of users who viewed one alternative as opposed to another. You will see a report similar to the one shown in Figure 10-7.

| User Type | Users | Revenue per User | Ecommerce Conversion Rate | Average QTY | Average Order Value | Transactions |
|---|---|---|---|---|---|---|
| **exp-2207684569 Original** | 1,167 % of Total: 10.75% (10,857) | $23.69 % of Total: 293.18% ($8.08) | 16.56% Site Avg: 5.30% (212.61%) | 2.23 Site Avg: 2.01 (10.93%) | $125.76 Site Avg: $120.03 (4.77%) | 234 % of Total: 32.01% (731) |
| **exp-2207684569 Variation1** | 1,139 % of Total: 10.49% (10,857) | $23.52 % of Total: 291.00% ($8.08) | 16.31% Site Avg: 5.30% (207.83%) | 2.15 Site Avg: 2.01 (6.77%) | $124.95 Site Avg: $120.03 (4.06%) | 227 % of Total: 31.05% (731) |
| 1. New Visitor | | | | | | |
| exp-2207684569 Original | 898 (72.30%) | $18.42 (77.73%) | 16.82% | 1.97 | $109.52 | 151 (64.53%) |
| exp-2207684569 Variation1 | 861 (71.39%) | $17.71 (75.31%) | 16.38% | 2.17 | $108.16 | 141 (62.11%) |
| 2. Returning Visitor | | | | | | |
| exp-2207684569 Original | 344 (27.70%) | $37.47 (158.15%) | 16.12% | 2.71 | $155.30 | 83 (35.47%) |
| exp-2207684569 Variation1 | 345 (28.61%) | $38.01 (161.61%) | 16.20% | 2.11 | $152.47 | 86 (37.89%) |

**Figure 10-7:** Report comparing the behavior of users who viewed different test pages

You can get the same results using Custom Dimensions. Just make sure the data is consistent—compare variation pageviews, conversion metrics, and other metrics between your Optimizely result panel and Google Analytics Custom Dimensions or Event Tracking-based reports.

# Analyzing Test Results

When you run a test, you have to do a post-test analysis to decide how to proceed. It's essential that you make sure your results are valid before ending them. But when exactly can you consider a test valid? Is it when your testing tool tells you that the results are statistically significant? The answer is no, *validity is not the same as significance.*

## Ending Your Tests

Suppose you run several A/B tests over the course of a year and many of them "win." Some tests show you that you will end up with a 25% uplift in revenue, or even higher. Yet, when you roll out the changes, the revenue does not increase 25%. And 12 months after running all those tests, the conversion rate is still pretty much the same. Why is this so?

The answer is that your uplifts were imaginary; there was no uplift to begin with. Yes, your testing tool said you had 95% statistical significance level or higher. Unfortunately, that doesn't mean much; statistical significance and validity are not the same. If you are not sure about the difference, check the post at `http://goo.gl/8HXNjp`.

Figure 10-8 shows a test results table, but looking at a summary screen like this is not enough. You can use these at-a-glance views for a quick check to see the overall status. However, you need to go beyond this once the test is valid and significant.

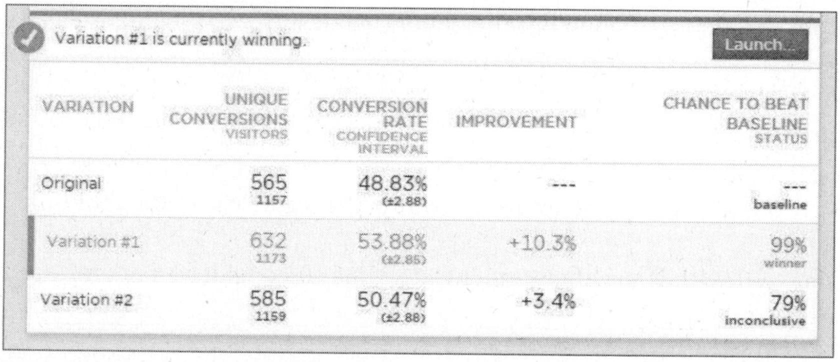

Variation #1 is currently winning. Launch...

| VARIATION | UNIQUE CONVERSIONS VISITORS | CONVERSION RATE CONFIDENCE INTERVAL | IMPROVEMENT | CHANCE TO BEAT BASELINE STATUS |
|---|---|---|---|---|
| Original | 565 1157 | 48.83% (±2.88) | --- | --- baseline |
| Variation #1 | 632 1173 | 53.88% (±2.85) | +10.3% | 99% winner |
| Variation #2 | 585 1159 | 50.47% (±2.88) | +3.4% | 79% inconclusive |

**Figure 10-8:** Test results table

Your test can really only end in three ways:

- Control wins
- No difference
- Variation(s) win(s)

Even when your testing tool tells you that you have reached the final verdict, your job isn't over. You need to conduct post-test analysis. In most cases, you need to do that *outside* of the testing tool. Sure, Optimizely enables you to see the results across predefined segments, but that's not enough either.

# Dealing with "No Significant Difference"

Suppose the overall outcome of your experiment is "no significant difference" between variations. Should you move on to something else straight away? *No, not so fast!* There are three important considerations you should keep in mind before discarding your initial hypothesis.

## The Hypothesis Was Right, But the Implementation Was Faulty

Suppose your qualitative research says that your potential customers have a deep concern about security. How many ways do you have to beef up the perception of security? Unlimited.

You might be on to something, but the way you did it was sub-optimal. If you have data that supports your hypothesis, try a few more iterations.

## There Was No Difference Overall, But the Variation Won Over the Original for Specific Segments

If you got a lift in returning visitors and mobile visitors, but a drop in new visitors and desktop users, those segments might cancel each other out. It might seem on the surface like it's a case of "no difference." Analyze your test across key segments to understand what's really going on.

Look at the test results at least across the following segments (make sure each segment has an adequate sample size):

- Desktop vs. tablet vs. mobile
- New vs. returning
- Traffic that lands directly on the page you're testing vs. traffic that came via an internal link

If your variation performed well with a specific segment, it's time to consider a personalized approach for that particular segment.

## There's No Difference, But You Like B Better than A

We're human beings, and we have personal preferences. So if your test says that there's no significant difference between variations, but you like B better, it's fine to stick with B.

If B is a usability improvement or represents your brand image better, go for it. But remember that those are *not* good reasons to go with B if B performs worse in a test.

## Summary

In this chapter you learned how to integrate your A/B testing data into Google Analytics using Optimizely as an example. If you perform tests on your website or app, you should definitely be able to analyze their performance on Google Analytics.

You also learned techniques that will help you end your tests more confidently. When a test output shows an increase (or decrease) in conversion rates for a specific variation, it is clear what you need to do; but what should you do if the test shows no significant difference? There are three important considerations to keep in mind before discarding your initial hypothesis:

1. The hypothesis was right, but the implementation was faulty.
2. There was no difference overall, but the variation won over the original for specific segments.
3. There is no difference, but you like B better than A.

Don't rely on a single source of data. Instead, go deeper than just looking at overall outcomes. You'll find more wins and have better data to make decisions. Integrating your testing tool with Google Analytics is an excellent way to go about it.

# 11 Email Data Integration

This chapter was contributed by Jim Gianoglio, Senior Digital Analyst at LunaMetrics. Jim works with implementation, analysis, and training of Google Analytics and Google Tag Manager. Before focusing on analytics, he led the SEO campaigns of Fortune 500 companies in the insurance, retail, and CPG industries. Jim has biked from Pittsburgh to Washington, D.C. in 41 hours, roasts coffee beans, and has done voiceovers for TV commercials.

It has always been a relatively simple task to track email campaign results in Google Analytics, as long as you include campaign parameters on your email link (as discussed in Chapter 1, "Implementation Best Practices," and Chapter 9, "Marketing Campaign Data Integration"). But this only measures sessions resulting from your email marketing; it does not measure when someone opens your email, which is an important interaction. It also does not enable you to measure user behavior across devices, which you might expect as users' emails can be linked back to unique IDs.

With some of the new features in Universal Analytics and the Measurement Protocol, however, this is now possible. In this chapter, you will learn two things you can do to bring your email data into Google Analytics, starting with tracking email opens, and moving into a more advanced implementation that enables you to use your email ID as a Google Analytics User ID.

## Tracking Email Opens

Email marketing is an important technique to keep customers engaged and initiate interactions with your business. As mentioned, it is rather simple to measure on-site behavior resulting from an email campaign. However, before users click through, you need to persuade them to open your email. By default, you will not see this information in Google Analytics, but following the steps in this chapter, you will be able to start understanding, for example, which email campaigns were more or less effective in grabbing your users' attention. Once you have this data, you can use it to create more successful subject lines that will lead to more opens and hopefully more interactions with your website.

To track email opens, you need to send information to Google Analytics every time an email is opened. This requires you to use the Measurement Protocol (discussed in Chapters 7 and 8).

You should also be comfortable working with UTM campaign parameters to track your marketing activities (you'll need to know this). For a refresher, read Chapter 9.

The following steps walk you through tracking email opens if you are using MailChimp (a popular email marketing solution). The same principles apply if you are using other email marketing solutions.

1. Create a Custom Metric.
2. Create an email campaign.
3. Add the Google Analytics code to your email.
4. Send your email and analyze the results.

## Step 1: Create a Custom Metric

In order to measure "opens," you need to create a new Custom Metric in the Google Analytics Admin interface for your property. This will enable Google Analytics to collect this data and recognize it as a new metric, which can subsequently be attributed to dimensions such as a campaign, country, or device type. A Custom Metric in Google Analytics requires both a property setting change and an addition to your hit during data collection (which you are sending in the HTTP request using the Measurement Protocol).

To set the Custom Metric, log in to Google Analytics and click on Admin at the top of your screen. Select the appropriate account and property and then click on Custom Definitions under the Property column. Then click on Custom Metrics.

In the next window, click on the + New Custom Metric button and give your Custom Metric a name, formatting type, and minimum and maximum values. Also make sure the box is checked for Active. I recommend the settings shown in Figure 11-1.

**Figure 11-1:** Custom Metric settings

After you create this Custom Metric, it will be assigned to the first open slot or index. If you use the standard version of Google Analytics, you have 20 slots available to store Custom Metrics; if you are a Google Analytics Premium client, you have 200 slots. In Figure 11-2, the Custom Metric is stored in Index 1. Remember this number, as you'll need to reference it later.

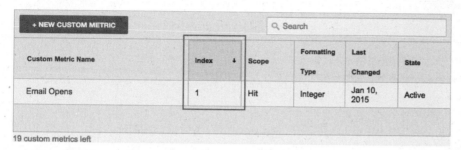

| + NEW CUSTOM METRIC | | Search | | | |
| --- | --- | --- | --- | --- | --- |
| Custom Metric Name | Index ↓ | Scope | Formatting Type | Last Changed | State |
| Email Opens | 1 | Hit | Integer | Jan 10, 2015 | Active |

19 custom metrics left

**Figure 11-2:** Custom Metric index

## Step 2: Create an Email Campaign

Next, you need to log in to your email marketing system and start a new email campaign. For this example, choose the Regular Ol' Campaign option shown in Figure 11-3 (if you are a MailChimp user).

Create Campaign ⌄

Regular Ol' Campaign

Plain-Text Campaign

A/B Split Campaign

RSS-Driven Campaign

Inbox Inspection

**Figure 11-3:** Creating an email marketing campaign

Proceed to build your email campaign by filling in all the details, including which list you're sending it to, the subject line, the reply-to address, and so on. Then you need to design your email by choosing your template or working from scratch to create the content of your email.

## Step 3: Add the Google Analytics Code to Your Email

Now the fun part—you need to add a snippet of code to your email. This is the code that will send the information to Google Analytics when the email is opened. In MailChimp, you can add a code block anywhere in your email. I suggest you add it to the bottom, but anywhere will work. You can add the code by clicking on the icon shown in Figure 11-4.

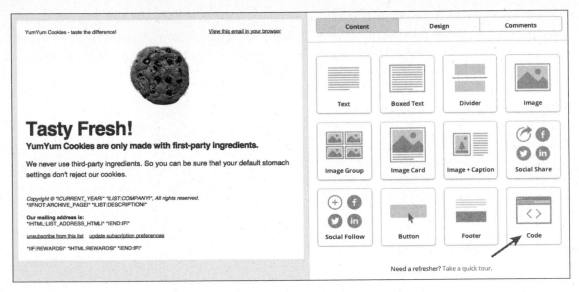

**Figure 11-4:** Adding a code block to your email in MailChimp

Now you need to edit the content of this block to include the following code:

```
<img src="http://www.google-analytics.com/collect?v=1&tid=UA-XXXXXXX-YY
    &cid=*|UNIQID|*&t=event&ec=email&ea=*|MC:SUBJECT|*&el=*|UNIQID|*
    &cs=newsletter&cm=email&cn=cookie-sale&cc=*|MC:SUBJECT|*&cm1=1" />
```

Here's what each piece of the code does:

- `img src`: Basically, you're fooling the email into thinking it has to load an image. There's no real image file, but the source that you specify is the `GET` request that sends your data to Google Analytics. So when your email tries to fetch the image, it's actually sending the data for you. Keep in mind that the email recipient has to allow images for this to work.

- `http://www.google-analytics.com/collect?`: This is the API endpoint for the Measurement Protocol. In layman's terms, this is where you're sending the data. The data that's being sent comes next, in the form of query parameters.

- `v=1`: Protocol version (required).

- `tid=UA-XXXXXX-YY`: Tracking ID and property ID (required). Please note that you will need to update this to show your own ID.

- `cid=*|UNIQID|*`: Client ID (required). This identifies a particular user, device, or browser. The `*|UNIQID|*` value is a dynamic parameter (also known as a merge tag) in MailChimp that will automatically fill in the user's MailChimp ID into the request.

- `t=event` : Hit type (required). This example uses event tracking, hence the event hit type.

- `ec=email`: Event category.

- `ea=*|MC:SUBJECT|*`: Event action. The `*|MC:SUBJECT|*` value will automatically populate the email's subject line into the request.
- `el=*|UNIQID|*`: Event label.
- `cs=newsletter`: Campaign source.
- `cm=email`: Campaign medium.
- `cn=cookie-sale`: Campaign name.
- `cc=*|MC:SUBJECT|*`: Campaign content. The `*|MC:SUBJECT|*` value will automatically populate the email's subject line into the request.
- `cm1=1`: Custom Metric 1. When you set up your Custom Metric in Step 1, whatever index your Custom Metric was stored in is the number you use here. For example, if your email opens Custom Metric was in index 8, you would use `cm8=1`.

**NOTE**    You can learn more about these parameters from the Measurement Protocol Parameter reference guide at `http://goo.gl/mUafDO`.

Keep in mind that you need to be consistent in your naming conventions for campaign source, medium, and content. Any links in your email that go to your site should be tagged with the same source, medium, and campaign. Following this example, your links would be tagged as follows:

```
www.yumyum.com/landing-page/?utm_source=newsletter&utm_medium=email
&utm_campaign=cookie-sale&utm_content=*|MC:SUBJECT|*
```

## Step 4: Send Your Email and Analyze the Results

Finish the remaining steps to create your email and send it. Then, log in to Google Analytics and open your Real Time reports to check how many people are opening your emails in real time! Note that you can see email opens in the Events menu and inbound traffic in the Traffic Sources menu located at the left sidebar of your Real Time reports, which can be found at `http://goo.gl/IK7sGt`.

When someone opens your email, it will record an Email Open metric, and you'll see this in your Events reports. This data will enable you to perform interesting analyses, such as identifying drop offs from opens to sessions and to purchases. This will empower you to make more informed decisions when it comes to creating subject lines that drive more opens, more sessions, and more interactions with your website. You can also create an email marketing dashboard, as shown in Figure 11-5.

With this tracking in place, when a user opens your email, an event hit is sent to Google Analytics, which causes a new session to start. That session will have no landing page (the first hit is an event, not a pageview). If they don't click through to your site, it will be a session with zero pageviews.

To prevent this from happening, you need to filter out these "email open" event hits from your main view. It is recommended you create a new view that includes only these hits to be able to see this data. To filter out these email open events, create a new filter with the settings shown in Figure 11-6. To include only these hits in the email-specific view, apply the same filter but change the name to *Include Email Opens* and select Include as the Filter Type.

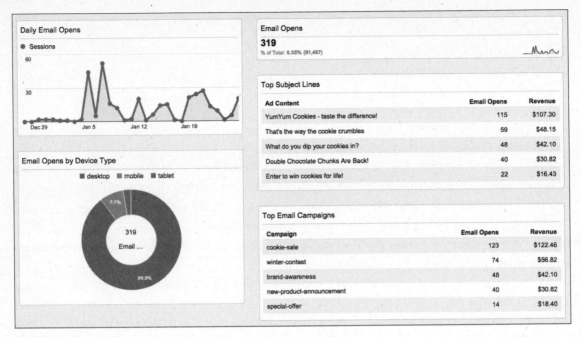

**Figure 11-5:** Email marketing dashboard in Google Analytics

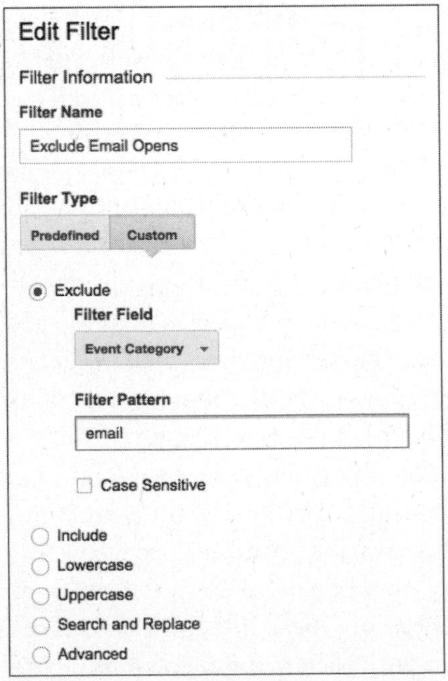

## Edit Filter

Filter Information

**Filter Name**

Exclude Email Opens

**Filter Type**

Predefined | Custom

◉ Exclude

**Filter Field**

Event Category ▾

**Filter Pattern**

email

☐ Case Sensitive

○ Include
○ Lowercase
○ Uppercase
○ Search and Replace
○ Advanced

**Figure 11-6:** Filtering email open events from your main view

# Tracking User Behavior Across Devices

One of the most powerful features of Universal Analytics is User ID. This lets you associate multiple sessions (and any activity within those sessions) with a unique ID. With it, you can get a more accurate user count, can analyze the signed-in user experience, and can access the Cross Device reports (as discussed in Chapter 8, "User Data Integration").

The challenge is that you don't always have a way to identify your users. For sites that require a log in, this is not a major problem. But for many sites, this is a high barrier to entry. Without a user logging in to your site, it's difficult to know who they are.

With email marketing, however, you have a way to identify your users. If someone has signed up for your newsletter or checked the box to be notified of special offers, at the very least you know their email address. And your email service provider likely has a unique identifier that you can use for the User ID.

Here are the steps you need to follow to track your users cross device behavior with their MailChimp IDs:

1. Set up a User ID view in Google Analytics.
2. Add the MailChimp ID to the links in your email.
3. Send the User ID to Google Analytics.

## USER ID AND PERSONALLY IDENTIFIABLE INFORMATION POLICIES

Note that according to Google Analytics Terms of Service, it is strictly forbidden to send Personally Identifiable Information to your Google Analytics account, and email addresses certainly fall under that category. You can use a unique identifier, such as MailChimp's ID, but not an email address.

In addition, all businesses using the User ID feature must adhere to the following policies:

1. You will not upload Personally Identifiable Information; if you do so, your Google Analytics account can be terminated, and you may lose your Google Analytics data.
2. You must make sure you have the full rights to use this service, to upload data, and to use it with your Google Analytics account.
3. You will give your end users proper notice about the implementations and features of Google Analytics you use (e.g., notice about what data you will collect via Google Analytics, and whether this data can be connected to other data you have about the end user). You will either get consent from your end users, or provide them with the opportunity to opt-out from the implementations and features you use.
4. If you use an SDK to implement any Google Analytics Advertising Features, such as Audience Reporting or Remarketing, you will abide by the Policy for Google Analytics Advertising Features, in addition to the Google Play Developer Program Policies, or any other applicable policy.

Source: http://goo.gl/x6tH9u

## Step 1: Set Up a User ID View in Google Analytics

Before you can start tracking your users' behavior across devices, you need to create a view that is User ID enabled. The User ID view is only available in Universal Analytics properties where User ID is enabled.

User ID views include a set of Cross Device reports that aren't available in other reporting views. These reports enable you to analyze how users engage with your content on different devices over the course of multiple sessions.

To create a User ID view, log in to your account and click on Admin at the top of your screen interface, then navigate to the appropriate account and property. In the Property column, click on Tracking Info and then User ID, as shown in Figure 11-7.

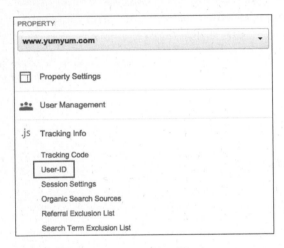

**Figure 11-7:** Creating a User ID view

Follow the steps for enabling the User ID feature, including reviewing and agreeing to the User ID policy, setting up the User ID, and creating a User ID view. Notice that during the process you will see a message regarding the nature of User ID views. In that message you will notice the following:

*A User-ID view is filtered. All reports in this view display data from sessions in which a User-ID is detected. Use a different view to see data from sessions in which a User-ID is not detected.*

For an in-depth explanation of User ID views and how to interpret the reports in them, please refer to Chapter 8.

## Step 2: Add the MailChimp ID to the Links in Your Emails

Since you already have a unique ID associated with the users who are on your email list, that's a good place to start. You simply need a way to dynamically insert each user's ID at the end of each link in the email that sends them to your site.

This is relatively easy to do in MailChimp. You just need to add a merge tag to the end of your links. For example, the following link:

```
www.yumyum.com/landing-page/?utm_source=newsletter&utm_medium=email
&utm_campaign=cookie-sale&utm_content=*|MC:SUBJECT|*
```

Would be updated to include the User ID as follows:

```
www.yumyum.com/landing-page/?utm_source=newsletter&utm_medium=email
&utm_campaign=cookie-sale&utm_content=*|MC:SUBJECT|*&mcid=*|UNIQID|*
```

That extra parameter, `mcid=*|UNIQID|*`, will automatically include the unique ID of any user who clicks through to your site from an email that you send them. The `mcid` is just a short term for MailChimp ID, and the `*|UNIQID|*` is a dynamic parameter (also known as a merge tag) in MailChimp that will fill in the user's MailChimp ID.

The end result is that when a user clicks on the link in your email, the URL of the page they land on will look similar to the following:

```
www.yumyum.com/landing-page/?utm_source=newsletter&utm_medium=email
&utm_campaign=cookie-sale&utm_content=YumYum%20Cookies%20%2d%20
taste%20the%20difference%12&mcid=7575debfd4
```

## Step 3: Send the User ID to Google Analytics

When a user lands on your site, you need to check if there's an `mcid` parameter in the URL. You'll be sending the value of this to Google Analytics as the User ID. But since the `mcid` parameter will only be present on the first pageview of the visit, you need a way to record that value for subsequent hits (pageviews, events, and so on) within the session. To do that, you need to store this value in a cookie. This is necessary because you need to set the User ID on all subsequent hits in the session after you have identified the user's ID.

So for every page that loads, you need to first check if there is a `mcid` parameter. If there is, set a cookie with that parameter and send it along to Google Analytics. If there's not a `mcid` parameter, you need to check to see if there's a cookie with the `mcid` value. If there is, you send that value to Google Analytics; otherwise, don't send any User ID.

Here's the code that performs those functions:

```
function getUserId() {
    var params = location.search;
    var mcid = params.match('mcid=(.*)');
    if(mcid) {  // if the mcid parameter is in the URL
        var uid = mcid[1];  // grab the value of the parameter
        setCookie('mcid', uid, 30);  // set a cookie named mcid with the
                                     // value of the mcid parameter and
                                     // an expiration of 30 minutes.
```

```
            return uid;
        }
        else {  // if there was no mcid parameter
            uid = getCookie('mcid');  // look for the mcid cookie
            return uid;  // will return the value of the mcid cookie, or if
                         // there is no mcid cookie will return an empty
                         // string
        }
    };

function setCookie(cname, cvalue, exp) {
    var d = new Date();
    d.setTime(d.getTime() + (exp*60*1000));
    var expires = "expires="+d.toUTCString();
    document.cookie = cname + "=" + cvalue + "; " + expires;
}

function getCookie(cname) {
    var name = cname + "=";
    var ca = document.cookie.split(';');
    for(var i=0; i<ca.length; i++) {
        var c = ca[i];
        while (c.charAt(0)==' ') c = c.substring(1);
        if (c.indexOf(name) == 0) {
            return c.substring(name.length,c.length);
        }
    }
    return "";
}

var userId = getUserId();  // sets a variable to the value of either
                           // the mcid parameter, the mcid cookie, or
                           // an empty string. This is what will be
                           // used in the Google Analytics <create>
                           // command
```

Note that you would also need to add the following bold code to your Google Analytics tracking node:

```
ga('create', 'UA-xxxxxxxx-y', 'auto', {'userId': userId});
ga('send', 'pageview');
```

## Bonus Step: Add a Custom Dimension with a User ID Value

Although you're sending the user's ID to Google Analytics for the purpose of the User ID view, this ID is not actually available as a dimension in any of your reports. To make sure you have access to this value in the reporting interface, you can send it to Google Analytics using a Custom Dimension in addition to sending it as the User ID value.

To do this, first you need to create a Custom Dimension in the Admin interface of Google Analytics for your property. Log in to Google Analytics and click on Admin at the top of your screen. Select the appropriate account and property and click on Custom Definitions under the Property column, as shown in Figure 11-8. Then click on Custom Dimensions.

PROPERTY

www.yumyum.com

- Property Settings
- User Management
- .js Tracking Info

PRODUCT LINKING

- AdWords Linking
- AdSense Linking
- All Products
- Remarketing
- Dd Custom Definitions
  - Custom Dimensions
  - Custom Metrics
- Dd Data Import
- Social Settings

**Figure 11-8:** Creating a Custom Dimension

In the next screen, click on the New Custom Dimension button. Give your Custom Dimension a name, set the scope to Hit, and make sure the box is checked for Active, as shown in Figure 11-9.

After you create this Custom Dimension, it will be assigned to the first open slot or index. If you use Universal Analytics (`analytics.js`), you have 20 slots available to store Custom Dimensions. If you are a Google Analytics Premium client, you will have 200 slots. In Figure 11-10, the Custom Dimension is stored in Index 1 (see the second column). Remember this number, as you'll need to reference it in the code.

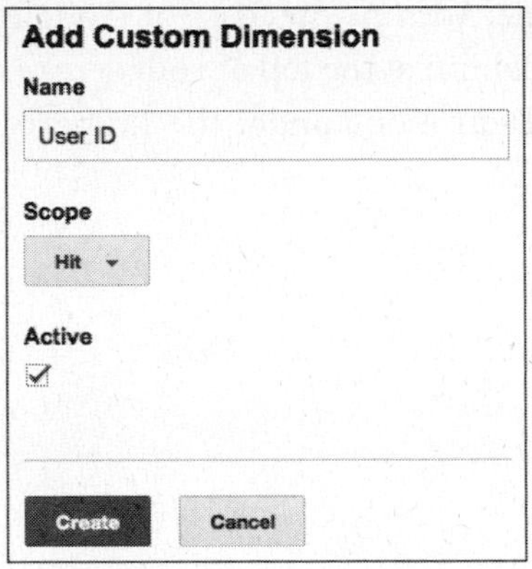

**Add Custom Dimension**

**Name**

User ID

**Scope**

Hit ▾

**Active**

☑

Create    Cancel

**Figure 11-9:** Custom Dimension settings

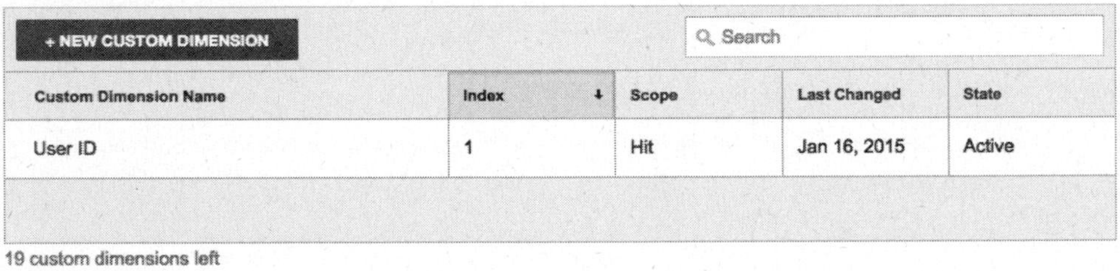

| Custom Dimension Name | Index ↓ | Scope | Last Changed | State |
|---|---|---|---|---|
| User ID | 1 | Hit | Jan 16, 2015 | Active |

+ NEW CUSTOM DIMENSION    🔍 Search

19 custom dimensions left

**Figure 11-10:** The Custom Dimension index number

Now all you need to do is add a single line to the last tracking code from Step 3 (see the bold line):

```
ga('create', 'UA-58403778-1', 'auto', {'userId': userId});
ga('set', 'dimension1', userId);
ga('send', 'pageview');
```

This line will set the Custom Dimension in slot 1 to the value of your `userId` variable. If your Custom Dimension happened to be in slot 8, your code would look like this:

```
ga('set', 'dimension8', userId);
```

Now you can select the User ID as a Secondary Dimension in Custom Reports, Segments, Dashboards, and more.

# Summary

In this chapter you learned two important email integrations: tracking email opens and using MailChimp ID as a User ID to measure cross-device behavior.

The first integration, tracking email opens, brings insightful data that will help you understand which email campaigns were more or less effective in grabbing your users' attention. Once you have this data, you can use it to create more successful subject lines that will lead to more opens and hopefully more interactions with your website. The following steps walk you through tracking email opens if you are using MailChimp, but the same principles apply if you are using other email marketing solutions.

1. Create a Custom Metric.
2. Create an email campaign.
3. Add the Google Analytics code to your email.
4. Send your email and analyze the results.

The second integration, Tracking User Behavior Across Devices, will provide a way to identify your users using MailChimp IDs. Below are the steps you need to follow to track your users' cross-device behavior with their MailChimp IDs:

1. Set up a User ID view in Google Analytics.
2. Add the MailChimp ID to the links in your email.
3. Send the User ID to Google Analytics.

Email marketing is a powerful technique to both engage users and initiate transactions, but it is also a great way to understand your customers and customize their interactions with your business. The integrations discussed in this chapter will help you with these endeavors.

# 12

# Offline Data Integration

As you have already learned in the previous chapters, Google Analytics provides a powerful way for developers to send requests to Google Analytics from anywhere: the Measurement Protocol. This is a powerful tool because it brings measurement to the next level, from websites and apps to any customer touch point.

In this chapter, you learn about a simple method to implement offline tracking that allows any marketer (unrelated to company size) to take advantage of it. Note that since the solution is very broad, and it was intended for anyone to use, it is somewhat manual. If you have developer resources and know-how, you can find a more automated (and therefore less error-prone) solution. The solution is built using a Google form and an App Script in order to send requests to Google Analytics using the Measurement Protocol.

The method discussed here is called Universal Analytics Form, a solution I developed with my colleague Eduardo Cereto Carvalho, Technical Product Expert on the Google Analytics team. The form is a simple solution for implementing the Measurement Protocol to upgrade your current tracking capabilities.

**NOTE** To learn more about how to create a Google form, visit `http://goo.gl/8pyOMy`. In addition, take a few minutes to read more about App Scripts, which is a JavaScript cloud scripting language that provides easy ways to automate tasks across Google products and third-party services and to build web applications. Learn more at `http://goo.gl/gQqJBe`.

## The Full Customer Journey

Suppose you offered coupons with discounts for store purchases on your website and invested money in online advertising. If that's the case, you should be really eager to understand whether the ad spending brought revenue to your store. This information will allow you to close the loop when it comes to attributing marketing dollars online to revenue offline.

In very general terms, this solution works by adding an identifier on your coupon when a person downloads it (let's say a User ID). This ID is then passed back to Google Analytics from your store via a simple Google form.

To use this solution, you need to convince your cashiers to fill in a short Google form to send the coupon number and other information to Google Analytics. *That might be no small task.* The form enables you to link the offline spending to acquisition channels (and other info) for any customer who downloaded that coupon. It is extremely important to keep in mind that Google Analytics Terms of Service strictly forbids adding personal identifiable information (PII) to your data collection, so make sure not to add names, surnames, usernames, social security numbers, and so on.

While it is not very difficult to add a coupon ID to the form and send information about the purchase to Google Analytics, it might be a bit more challenging to create a User ID that can link all the information. The recommended approach is to create a User ID for the customer the moment he or she downloads the coupon and have this same ID printed on the coupon. This way, the cashier could add it to the form and the full customer journey would be available from within Google Analytics.

If the person downloading the coupon is already registered with your company, you should use the User ID that's already assigned to the person, as explained in Chapter 8, "User Data Integration." If you have no User ID, you could set a random number to the person, which would be used to link between the online and offline sessions.

**NOTE** This approach can also be used to integrate call center data to your Google Analytics data, using a process similar to the steps described in this chapter. However, instead of printing an ID on a coupon, the person answering the call would request the ID from the caller. This can be done by asking the visitor to click on a button on the site that accesses the Client ID on Google Analytics and shows a popup with that number. To learn more about retrieving the Client ID, visit `http://goo.gl/0hxMiE`.

# Implementation Details and Script

This section includes an example of a fictitious website that advertises online and directs visitors to a website where they can download a discount coupon for the brick-and-mortar store. The following steps are required in order to implement the Universal Analytics Form solution.

1. Define your data collection needs.
2. Create the Google form.
3. Add and edit the script to match your needs.
4. Add a trigger.
5. Make sure the form is being filled.

## Step 1: Define Your Data Collection Needs

Think profoundly about which pieces of information you need to collect in order to measure your goals. You may want to revisit Chapter 1, "Implementation Best Practices," where you learned about planning your implementation and the Web Analytics process in general.

Remember that for each piece of information you request, you need a field in the form. The more cumbersome this form becomes, the less likely the cashiers will fill it in completely or correctly. Read through the Measurement Protocol parameter reference to learn more about all the options available to you at `http://goo.gl/PfX6Ra`.

# Step 2: Create the Google Form

Create a Google form at `http://goo.gl/0mQHQM` and add one question to collect each data point that you need. This form will define which data will be collected and where it will be displayed on your Google Analytics reports. The form created from this chapter's example script would look similar to Figure 12-1.

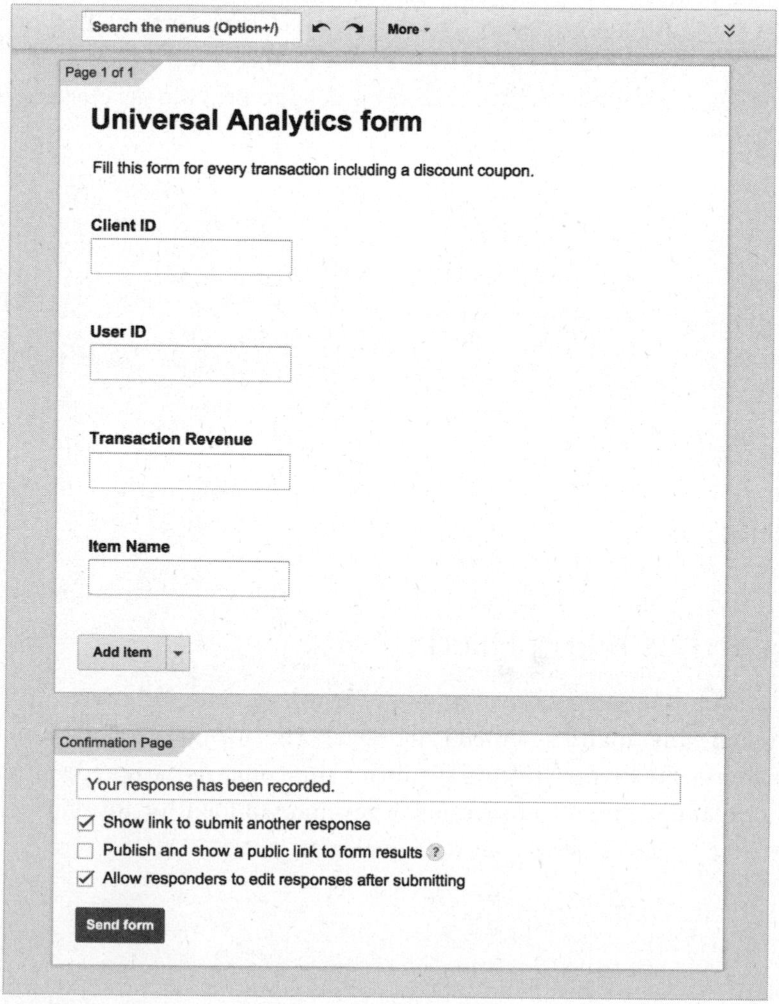

**Figure 12-1:** Form created from sample script

## Step 3: Add and Edit the Script to Match Your Needs

On the menu above your form, click on Tools and then Script Editor. Paste the following script into your Script Editor (you can find a text version at http://goo.gl/YEkO5V). Edit the script to match your data collection needs. You can learn about each part of the script and what it does in the comments in the script. Don't forget to change the Property ID on the script. Click Save.

Set up Custom Dimensions on the Google Analytics interface to work with any custom data you decide to collect (if you decide to use Custom Dimensions). It might be helpful to read the article explaining Custom Dimensions at http://goo.gl/7bwI6T.

## Step 4: Add a Trigger

Add a trigger for the script to run every time a form is submitted. On the Script page, click on Resources and then on All Your Triggers. Click on "No triggers set up. Click here to add one now." Then click on Save for the default trigger (shown in Figure 12-2). You need to provide permissions for the app. Finally, click OK.

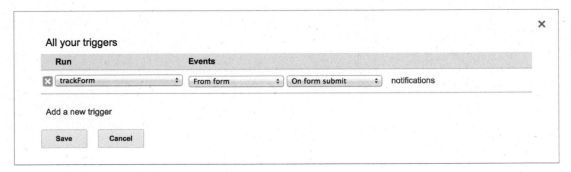

**Figure 12-2:** Universal Analytics form trigger

## Step 5: Make Sure the Form Is Being Filled

As mentioned, since this solution was built to serve a broad number of professionals and companies from small to large, this process is somewhat manual, which is not ideal. This means it will be your job to educate and check that employees are actually filling the form. You could use any reporting available to you from your store (for example, total transactions or revenue) to identify any gaps in data collected from the form. This is critical to ensure your data quality.

# And Finally...The Script!

Here is the script that you will need to copy to your form. You can find a text version at http://goo.gl/YEkO5V.

```javascript
var GA_TRACKING_ID = 'UA-xxxxxxxx-y';

// maps each form field to a field in GA
var data_mapping = {
 0: 'cid',    // Client ID
 1: 'uid',    // User ID
 2: 'tr',     // Transaction Revenue
 3: 'in',     // Item Name
}

function trackForm(e) {
 var data = [],
      item,
      res = e.response.getItemResponses();

 for (var i=0; i< res.length; i++){
      item = res[i].getItem();
   if(data_mapping[item.getIndex()]) {
      data.push([
      data_mapping[item.getIndex()],
      res[i].getResponse()
    ]);
  }
 }

 data.push(

   ['tid', GA_TRACKING_ID],    // Uses the ID you provided in
                               // the beginning of the Script.

   ['v'  , '1'],    // The protocol version.

// ['cid', Math.floor(Math.random()*10E7)],
// Remove the backslashes at the beginning of the line above
// if you don't have a Client ID, this will set a random value.

   ['t'  , 'transaction'],    // Hit type must be one of the following:
                              // 'pageview', 'appview', 'event',
                              // 'transaction', 'item', 'social',
                              // 'exception', 'timing'.

   ['ti', Math.floor(Math.random()*10E7)],    // Assigns a randon value
```

```
                                                // to Transaction ID.

  ['z'  , Math.floor(Math.random()*10E7)]   // Cache Buster.

);

var payload = data.map(function(el){return el.join('=')}).join('&');

var options =
  {
    'contentType': 'application/json',
    'method' : 'post',
    'payload' : payload
  };

UrlFetchApp.fetch('http://www.google-analytics.com/collect', options);
}
```

Once you finish the implementation and people start filling in the form, your data will start being populated into Google Analytics. The resulting reports will depend on what data you will be sending to Google Analytics, but if you are sending, for example, revenue and User ID, your revenue per user will be updated in Google Analytics reports.

# Summary

In this chapter you learned how to integrate offline interactions within Google Analytics using a simple solution, which is meant to show that sending offline data into Google Analytics is not rocket science. Since this method is intended for any business (at any level), it is somewhat manual, not requiring too much development.

The Universal Analytics Form discussed in this chapter requires you to use the Measurement Protocol and follow the following steps:

1. Define your data collection needs.
2. Create the Google form.
3. Add and edit the script to match your needs.
4. Add a trigger.
5. Make sure the form is being filled.

Closing the loop between online and offline is extremely important in order to analyze the performance of your marketing, and through this solution you will have a 360 degree view of your marketing investment and customer behavior.

Happy Analyzing!

# Index